Hamlyn a

Colin Gamble

Freshwater Fishing

illustrated by Glenn Steward,
Roger Hall and Sam Peffer

Hamlyn
London · New York · Sydney · Toronto

FOREWORD

Freshwater angling, in its many forms, is already acknowledged to be by far the most popular participant sport in the British Isles, as in several other countries, and in spite of a heavy demand on many fisheries continues to attract new enthusiasts at a growing rate.

To be consistently successful an angler needs more than suitable tackle and skill in handling it. It is more important that he should have a deep knowledge of the haunts and habits of the species he seeks and an unswerving enthusiasm to catch them.

Within the limitations of this relatively small book will be found, in text and illustration, the information on tackle, baits, methods and the habits of fish which will take a beginner to competence at least.

C.G.

Published by The Hamlyn Publishing Group Limited
London · New York · Sydney · Toronto
Astronaut House, Feltham, Middlesex, England

Copyright © The Hamlyn Publishing Group Limited 1972
Reprinted 1974, 1975, 1976
ISBN 0 600 31662 9

Photoset by BAS Printers Limited, Hampshire
Colour separations by Schwitter Limited, Zurich
Printed in Spain by Mateu Cromo, Madrid

CONTENTS

FRESHWATER FISHING

Introduction

In most parts of the world fishing for the salmons and trouts is accorded a higher esteem than is fishing for other freshwater species. It is more rigorously controlled and more effectively managed, often has an aura of mystique and purism, and may, indeed, be socially more acceptable.

The British term 'coarse fishing', used to describe angling for all but the game species, is a particularly inappropriate one, embracing as it does many forms of angling which demand of the angler a high degree of dexterity and delicacy. This term has, for the uninformed, a connotation of clumsiness and crudity which is completely false.

Let no angler feel inferior in any way because he fishes only for the 'coarse' species. If he is a good angler his skills do not in any way fall short of those of the game angler, and his knowledge must extend to a far wider range of species, conditions, methods of presentation and types of water.

To some extent this term is being superseded by 'sport fishing', which much better describes the almost peculiarly British approach of striving to catch fish, caring for them solicitously, and returning the great majority of them to the water.

Names, however, are not important; what matters is that one should enjoy the fishing and happy indeed is the man, an angler without any reservation or qualification, who can fish with equal enthusiasm for small canal roach or huge lake pike, for tiny dace, massive carp, and find happiness merely in angling. Such a man is a real angler.

He will find that the skills and knowledge which he develops in one branch of his angling are complementary to those of other branches. The broader the range of his angling, the better angler he is likely to be in all branches, for there is more to angling than tackle and baits and methods. There is, as the ultimate ability, a sympathetic tuning-in to the world under water, and with this an angler will catch any kind of fish, anywhere.

The fight is over and the sport fisher returns his catch

Success can depend on a knowledge of the underwater world

The approach to angling

The most valuable ability an angler can have is to be able to look over a stretch of river or a pool, to consider what he sees, along with weather conditions, season of year, light conditions, etc., and then to predict where the fish will be. The best of anglers can do this, if not infallibly, at least with enough success to lift their results out of the common run. They start with the advantage of putting the bait where there are fish, or where fish will come.

A great wealth of background experience is needed to make such predictions with any confidence, and this comes only to those with an observing eye and an enquiring mind. Time which is spent in looking at fish or for fish is never wasted: this is how one learns what conditions and features attract them, how, when and where they feed and what they eat. This knowledge is as vital a part of the angler's equipment as his rod and line.

There is a skill in looking into water, a skill which increases with practice. This is important, not only because it sometimes allows one to see the fish one seeks to catch, but also because it encourages one to be concerned about the submerged part of the tackle, the part whose behaviour is most important in the catching of fish.

It is no coincidence that the best of anglers are usually knowledgeable naturalists, that some are acknowledged authorities on subjects which relate to fish life. All anglers can only benefit from such study.

It should always be remembered that a fish is well equipped to avoid danger, some species particularly so. They have senses of an acuteness far beyond the senses of man, senses which allow them to detect the unusual and the alarming, and most fish are also quite capable of learning by experience that that which once fooled them is best avoided in the future.

The angler should always regard his fish as sensitive wild creatures which are alert for any sign of danger. His efforts to catch them will succeed consistently only if they are regarded as a contest between the wits of man and the senses and instincts of the fish.

The lateral line, an important part of a fish's defences

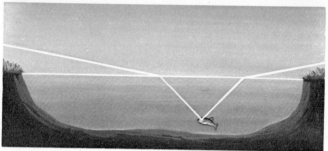

The window of vision of a fish

Any angler of experience will confirm that it is always the larger fish of a species which are most easily alarmed and which remain longest in that state. The higher your ambitions, therefore, the more important it is that you should take great care to cause no alarm to the fish.

The degree of importance attaching to this point varies to some extent between the species, but this is no reason to relax caution at any time. Numberless fish remain uncaught through lack of caution but no angler ever missed a fish through being too quiet.

Obviously the greatest care is called for when fishing close at hand in small, clear waters. It is then absolutely essential that the angler should be screened by reeds or bushes, that he should keep low, that he should be dressed unobtrusively, that he should move as little as possible and then slowly and lightly.

Even when fishing at some distance it is unwise to risk disturbing the nearer water for there is a communication between fish which can spread alarm through a wide stretch of water.

Never make the mistake of thinking that because you cannot see the fish they cannot see you. However deep and murky the water may be, the silhouette of an angler will cause a detectable reduction in the amount of light reaching the fish.

Even the slender silhouette of a rod is enough to scare away fish from the near bank, and the flash from a highly varnished rod is plain to see at a great distance. Rods are best finished with a matt surface.

Water transmits vibrations very efficiently and fish are very sensitive to such warnings. To move carelessly, to bang tackle on the bank, to knock in rod rests etc., will surely mean that you have, at least temporarily, driven the fish away.

Particular situations may call for very special precautions. For instance, if you stalk chub in a small clear stream, it is a perfectly reasonable precaution to camouflage the face with a net veil as used in pigeon shooting, for there may well be less than a rod length between angler and fish. More usually, simple common-sense caution and thoughtfulness is enough to avoid the commonest cause of poor catches.

Quite the most important decision an angler has to make

A wise angler keeps low and screened, avoiding the skyline

comes when he chooses the spot where he will fish. No other decision dictates so absolutely what his results will be.

To the beginner all parts of rivers and pools look much alike and equally likely to hold fish. However, fish are never spread evenly through the water, indeed it would usually be true to say that something like ten per cent of the water holds ninety per cent of the fish.

Especially in rivers, where there is frequent fluctuation in current, in direction, speed and depth, and where the nature of the bed can change several times in a few yards, the species are largely separated, occupying clearly defined stretches whose character meets their individual tastes.

Some overlapping of species does occur, of course, resulting in mixed bags, but the most successful angling invariably starts with a particular species in mind, with the location, the bait and the method chosen as most likely to produce that species. Merely to choose a comfortable and convenient spot and there to fish for whatever may chance to come along often means that nothing does come.

A valuable ability is that of 'reading the water'

Every angling session, whether it ends in outstanding success or dismal failure, is an opportunity to learn a little more about what does and what does not attract fish. Careful note should be taken of the depth of the swim and of surrounding areas. Look out for gravel spits, ledges, gulleys in the bed, any abrupt change in depth, and note the incidence of snails, shrimps, fry and other food items.

Take note also of weed growth of all kinds, submerged and emergent, for very often plant growth determines where fish will concentrate. Weed beds offer concealment and safety, they provide relief from strong currents, they act as traps for water-borne food items and as host to many of the small organisms upon which fish feed.

After some years, perhaps many years, of thoughtful experience in a variety of waters and conditions, an angler should have accumulated a fund of first-hand knowledge which equips him to 'read' the water, forecasting which areas will hold which species, and to be right more often than he is wrong. When he is able to do this he is half way to success before he even sets up his tackle.

Rods

The rod must fulfil four separate functions. It has to cast the bait efficiently, allow adequate control of the tackle thereafter, deliver an effective strike, and absorb the energy of the fish after hooking. The relative importance of these jobs varies in different forms of angling and it is sometimes necessary to accept some deficiency in one respect to gain in another.

Anglers have always argued about their rods—their length, weight, action, material, etc.—but all would agree that the best rod for any kind of angling is the one with which one fishes effectively, with comfort and confidence, and this can vary between anglers according to physique, habit and sometimes to illogical prejudice.

It is possible, however, to define the broad characteristics of rods suited to different branches of angling and to specify a basic minimum armoury of rods which would permit effective participation in most kinds of freshwater fishing. It is a miserable experience to attempt to fish with totally inadequate or unsuitable tackle. A basic set of rods might comprise:

1. A 'general' rod of around

11–12 feet, with the action confined largely to the upper third of its length. This will give accurate casting of light tackle and a fast strike, and will afford pleasant and safe handling of the smaller species when used with lines of 1–3 lb. breaking strain. A vast choice of such rods is available in light hollow glass.

2. A rod of medium weight, in either glass or built cane, about 10 feet long and having an easy action right down to the hand. This is a splendid rod for general legering and is extremely efficient in tiring the more powerful species when used with lines in the range 4–7 lb. breaking strain. It is also a fine rod for casting lures up to about $\frac{1}{2}$ ounce weight.

3. A powerful rod, 9–10 feet long, capable of casting sizeable live or dead fish baits and heavy lures on lines of around 10 lb. breaking strain.

Regarding these rods as the nucleus of his armoury the beginner will be able to try his hand at just about every kind of fishing which comes his way, appreciate the virtues and deficiences of his rods, and make an informed choice of the additional rods he will inevitably acquire as his experience expands.

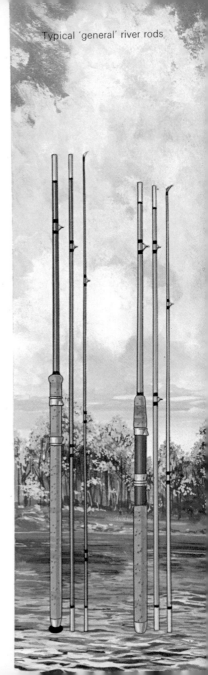

Typical 'general' river rods

Reels

By far the most important reel to the modern freshwater angler is the fixed spool type—indeed there are very many who neither possess nor use any other and find no deficiency.

For a very modest price a reel can be obtained which incorporates the sophistications of quick-change spools, optional ratchet, adjustable drag and anti-reverse gear. Such reels are of durable and practical design, are simple to use and maintain and give effortless casting with a fast recovery rate. With a couple of spare spools carrying line of assorted strengths one reel can cope very well with almost every type of freshwater fishing.

The versatile fixed spool reel and a centre pin reel

Nevertheless, there is still a place in many anglers' kits for a centre-pin reel, and the best of these, used for those jobs for which they are suited, are still beautifully efficient items. This type of reel is seen at its best when the hands of an expert feed off line to match the current's pull, sending a controlled bait to search the currents twenty, thirty and more yards downstream. Boat fishing, when long casting is not usually called for, offers a good chance to enjoy the more direct contact between angler and fish which this type of reel gives.

The multiplier, either a simple model or one with considerable mechanical refinement, is the choice of many anglers for the fishing of live and dead baits and the casting of heavy lures. A really good multiplier, though expensive, is a real joy to use. A poor one is an abomination.

Some anglers have a preference for the closed face reel for general use. This is essentially a fixed-spool reel with the spool and recovery mechanism enclosed within a housing. Their main advantage is their press-button, single-handed control over the release and engagement of the recovery

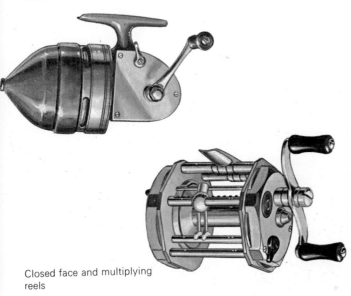

Closed face and multiplying
reels

mechanism; their main disadvantage, so many think, is the somewhat 'woolly' feel when in contact with a fish.

Lines and Hooks
The modern monofilament line is, quite rightly, the automatic choice for practically all freshwater fishing, and probably represents the greatest single advance in tackle over the last few decades.

It is not easy to make an objective comparison between

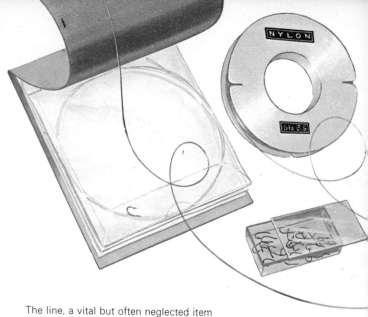

The line, a vital but often neglected item

brands. What the angler should do is to stick to a brand he knows so that he appreciates its qualities as regards suppleness, stretch, knotting properties, and so on, and can use it accordingly.

In spite of its durability, line should be tested frequently, especially the terminal few yards, for this is affected by the strains of casting and is abraded in use. Furthermore, although it may appear to have suffered no change it can sometimes abruptly and completely lose its nature and strength.

Braided lines are much softer in nature and are excellent for use on multiplying reels for they have no tendency to spring off the reel.

Hooks are available in a bewildering variety of sizes, shapes, sections, and finishes, either ready whipped to a length of nylon, with a spade end for whipping, or eyed. Whatever one advises on choice of hooks will inevitably run counter to some section of opinion, so I will merely quote my own practice and leave others to choose theirs.

On the rare occasions when I feel the need for a hook

smaller than UK size 16, I use one ready whipped. For all other sizes I use a round bend, medium length shank, straight eyed hook, slightly forged at the bend. These are fixed direct to the reel line with a four-fold blood knot.

I take the trouble to test the temper of a hook before using it and check that the eye is properly closed and smoothly formed. It is extreme folly to skimp care and attention to hooks and lines; they are, after all, the most vital items so far as landing fish is concerned.

Somewhat specialised designs of hooks are available incorporating features which are generally accepted to give some advantage for particular jobs. The benefits are very slight in most cases, and debatable in some, as one chooses between shank lengths, gape width, offset points, barbless, gilt, silver, bronze or blue finish, and so on.

Give me a hook of suitable size, that is well-formed, well-tempered and sharp, and I am confident of catching fish on it.

Selection of hooks and methods of attachment

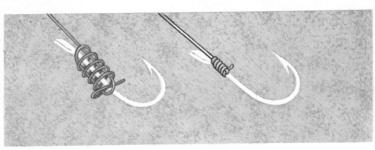

Floats

To most freshwater fishermen floats have a fascination of their own which leads to their collection in needlessly large numbers and constant experimenting in materials and designs.

The truth is that most float fishing can be done perfectly well with a traditional quill float in various sizes. A few feathers from crow, goose, turkey, and a length of peacock quill which can be cut into suitable lengths, will provide floats for a great deal of fishing.

There are conditions, though, which call for a rather specialised float. A powerful flow of water demands a float which will carry a shot load enough to ensure that the bait is held well down in the water. A suitable float will have a body of cork, balsa or elder pith fitted on a stem of quill or wood.

In windy conditions, when the waves on exposed lakes would toss floats about, a very long float with a buoyant body, or twin bodies, low down, and only a slim antenna emergent, will stand securely. The line is attached at the bottom only and is submerged to avoid wind drag.

Fluted and cork bodied floats, grayling float, quill floats

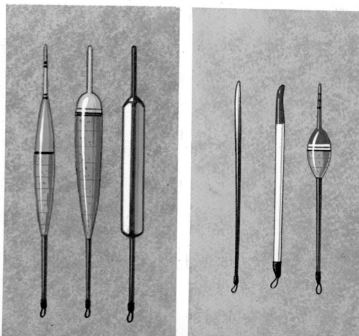

The method of long trotting, in which contact with the float must be maintained at long distances down lively currents, is carried out most effectively with a substantial float which has deep vertical flutings cut into the body. This permits the tackle to be controlled without significant deviation from its course.

When float fishing a live bait for pike, the float, though necessarily of substantial size, should be of a slim shape rather than bulbous. This encourages mobility of the bait and offers less drag to a biting fish. Two small floats in tandem are better than one very large one.

Sliding floats, which allow the bait to be fished at a depth greater than the length of the rod, must be fitted with very small rings, only just large enough for free passage of the line or they do not operate smoothly.

The prime consideration when choosing a float must usually be that it carries the amount of weight needed for proper bait presentation according to the conditions. All other considerations are secondary.

Further selection of floats

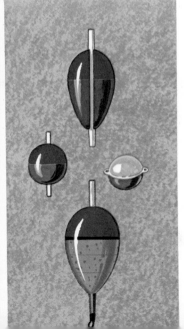
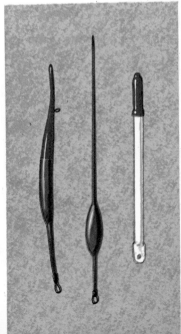

It must always be remembered that the most important factor in deciding a float's response to a delicate bite is the volume of the emergent tip. This should always be as small as possible, consistent with adequate visibility.

Accessories

The many accessories of angling, some quite essential, others mere trimmings, are available in a vast range of types and patterns. In some cases the choice is a matter of mere personal preference, in others there are important considerations to have in mind. For many anglers there is a very real pleasure and satisfaction in making many items themselves.

Landing Nets: The larger the fish, the more important is the landing net. Therefore let your landing net be really large in the frame, with a sectional or telescopic handle which will permit its use in awkward situations.

Keep Nets: Most experienced anglers agree that UK regional regulations governing the size of keep nets are inadequate to

Suitable accessories make for more enjoyable sport

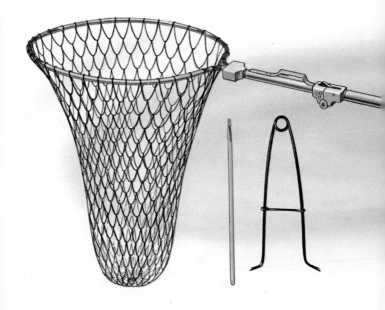

ensure the well-being of retained fish. Those who are concerned that their catch should be returned without harm will use a keep net very much larger than the permitted minimum and will retain fish for short periods only.

Rod Rests: A forked stick, though traditional, makes a very poor rod rest. It is better to purchase a rod rest of good design than to use a stick.

Seats and Containers: The traditonal seat-basket is still a popular choice though it is becoming more difficult to obtain a really well-made one. A well-designed seat-haversack is a commodious and comfortable alternative. It is better to carry a folding canvas chair than to sit in discomfort: to be uncomfortable or insecure is usually to fish badly.

Disgorgers: A pair of surgical forceps will find a score of uses apart from removing hooks as least as well as any other tool.

Tackle Containers: To hold the many small items—floats, weights, hooks, shot, lures, etc.—a multi-section cantilever box is ideal, giving neat storage with ease of access. The hook container should be lined with rubber foam to preserve hook points.

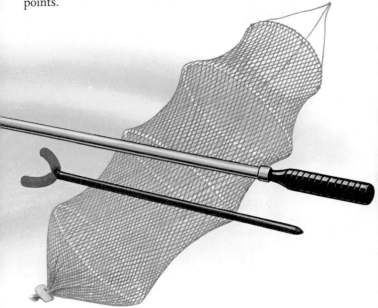

Worms are a fine bait for most species

Baits

It is a measure of the effectiveness of worms as bait that one could quite sensibly and profitably use them, at least some of the time, for every species.

Three kinds of worm are of particular interest to the angler, of which the lobworm is foremost. This worm is found lying out on lawns and borders after dark on calm, warm nights, when a dim light and a light tread will provide a supply.

These make a fine bait for chub, perch, bream, and tench, and for carp in some pools. They should be fished on a fairly large hook, size 8 to size 2 according to the species, the hook being passed once through the centre of the worm. The tail of a lobworm is a fine bait for large roach.

Two smaller worms of about equal importance to the angler are the cockspur and the brandling. The former is noticeably red, sometimes irridescent at the tail, and commonly occurs at a length between one and two inches. It is found in profusion in vegetable compost and is readily encouraged by laying damp sacking in a shady place.

Brandlings are found in manure heaps, are banded in red and yellow with a yellow tip to the tail, and give off an objectionable fluid when disturbed. This, however, does not deter most species of fish from eating them freely.

Very many anglers rely almost exclusively on commercially bred maggots for their baits; others breed less common varieties of fly larvae in meat and offal of various kinds. Of almost equal popularity is the pupa, when it sinks in water.

These baits need a small hook if fished singly, a size 18 or 20 being a popular choice, but maggots can be bunched on a larger hook for chub, tench, carp, bream and barbel.

Maggots can be coloured by incorporating a dye in their feed and anglers have individual preferences for colours and combinations of colours.

All species of fish will eat maggots, especially when they have been fed loose into the swim, but though this universal appeal is sometimes an attraction, it makes maggots of doubtful value to the angler who has set his sights upon the larger species. Although chub, barbel and carp will eat maggots

All species of fish will eat maggots

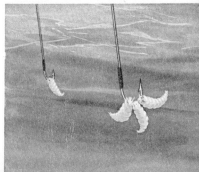

Baits of bread, sausage, luncheon meat and cheese

freely, they can be scared away by the catching of smaller fish which are inevitably also attracted.

A loaf of bread will supply a variety of baits invaluable for every species but the predators.

To use it as 'flake', merely tear off a piece of crumb from a very fresh loaf, fold it around the hook shank, and squeeze so as to leave the hook point in the fluffy part.

Large pieces of crust can be torn off, smaller baits are best cut as cubes. In either case the hook should be passed through the crust side to lie in the crumb. Hooks need to be reasonably large or they may tear out of this soft bait.

Crust is supreme as a floating bait for chub, carp, rudd, and sometimes for tench, and is a fine bait for bottom-feeding species if a shot is placed very near to the bait so as to tether it just above the bed.

Paste is made by briefly immersing stale bread in cold water and kneading with the fingers to the right consistency. To be fully effective paste should be soft enough to leave the hook when the tackle is retrieved. Firmer paste is likely to prevent effective hooking.

A balanced bait, half paste, half crust, which will only just sink, and hence will not become buried in soft weed or silt, is very effective for carp.

Several species, chub especially, are much attracted to fatty or meaty baits. Cubes of luncheon meat do very well, as do suet, fat bacon, tripe, and sausage meat.

Cheese is a very popular and often very productive chub bait, though most other species will also accept it. Soft processed cheese is convenient to use, though all cheeses are attractive to fish.

Cheese may be worked into a soft bread paste and will make a very attractive bait for all but the predators.

Strongly smelling cheese may be an advantage when the water is heavily coloured and baits are less readily visible.

Further selection of useful baits

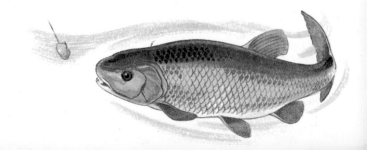

Stewed wheat, an excellent bait for roach, bream and chub
Earwigs, woodlice, etc. attract all smaller species, mussels are good
baits for carp and tench

With a loaf of bread in his bag, an angler can confidently approach many waters and catch fish of many species.

Many seeds come naturally to the fish in most waters and are eaten by most species. A range of baits is available for use with the smaller species, some cereals, some pulse seeds, all effective, few widely used.

Stewed wheat is a splendid bait, especially for roach, but only slightly less so for bream, tench and chub. One grain on a size 14 hook is ideal for roach, two or three grains on a slightly larger hook for the other species.

Hempseed is a small bait for the roach and dace specialist. When fed into the stream lightly but frequently, hempseed can induce a pre-occupation which makes other baits useless.

Peas and several kinds of bean seeds have been used as bait for roach, chub and bream with good effect, though not until quite lengthy pre-feeding had been carried out to accustom the fish to these items.

It is possible to mention only a few of the insects, larvae, etc., which have proved very attractive to fish of most species. It can safely be said that anything which crawls, wriggles or swims will be eaten by fish if presented properly.

Caddis larvae are eaten greedily by all fish, large and small, and they make wonderful baits fished singly for the small species, in bunches for the larger, with or without their cases. They are readily obtainable from the bed of practically any water, running or still.

Woodlice, earwigs and freshwater shrimps make excellent baits for roach and dace fished on fine tackle in clear water.

Wasp grubs, fished singly, in bunches, or in a chunk of comb, are deadly for chub, especially in the larger rivers where chub gather in shoals. Large slugs and snails will attract chub anywhere.

The flesh of freshwater mussels will attract most species, a whole mussel being used for carp and large tench, and smaller pieces for lesser fish.

Roach, chub and barbel will take peas and beans. Caddis larvae are fine roach baits, snails are good for chub

All species eat smaller fish at some times

The larvae of the chironomid flies, to be found in the bottom mud of absolutely any scrap of water and generally known as bloodworms are certainly eaten by every fresh-water species with the probable exception of pike. Their use as bait is generally restricted to the small species, very small, fine wire hooks being needed to present the bait.

Every species of fish will prey upon smaller fish at least some of the time, but it is profitable to use small fish as bait only for those species which are consistently piscivorous.

A bleak, a minnow, a gudgeon or a loach, with a sizeable hook through both lips, makes a splendid bait for casting dead to large chub. It requires no added weight and is best left to roll naturally down the current. It has the advantage that it is unlikely to be taken by a small fish.

The same fish baits, used live or dead, fished on float or leger tackle or given movement by a more active style, will appeal equally to perch in both rivers and lakes, while the gudgeon makes a good bait for pike and eels. Two small live minnows on the same hook provide a particularly effective bait for perch since there is no tendency to lie still on the bed.

Barbel, not usually regarded as predators, will feed very well on minnows, especially when some have been sent down the stream in advance.

Water which holds crayfish will surely be clean and healthy. If it also holds chub they are likely to grow to large sizes. A crayfish makes a splendid bait for them, hooked through the second segment from the tail with a large hook and legered with as little weight as possible.

The catfish, the pike-perch and the eel are all scavengers which will pick up a dead fish from the bed. Any small fish of suitable size is useful for this method.

It is, of course, with pike that fish baits come really to the fore, for apart from articifial lures and freak catches this is the only way of taking them. Any species locally available will attract pike, and sea fish are accepted freely.

Whilst it is true that large pike may be taken on small fish baits, the converse is rarely true. To a large extent, therefore, one can fish selectively.

A true predator, the pike feeds almost entirely on fish

Groundbaiting, often essential for large catches

Groundbaiting

By no means all freshwater fishing demands groundbaiting, indeed in some conditions to use groundbait would almost ensure failure. It is important, therefore, to be clear when to use groundbait and to understand what it can be expected to achieve.

Groundbaiting consists of providing food, or sometimes merely conditions which lead the fish to suppose there is the possibility of food, in an endeavour to make the area being fished more attractive to the fish and thus to cause a concentration of fish there.

Groundbaiting is not a process which should be used habitually, without thought, without taking into consideration the habits and numbers of the species being sought, the nature of the water and the method in use. Merely to mix up a bag of proprietary groundbait and throw it in when fish are proving elusive, is to invite disappointment.

Most proprietary mixtures consist largely or entirely of finely ground breadcrumb which produces a cloud in the water as it sinks, as it breaks up on the bed, or as it rolls down the current. This will itself attract and hold fish which feed on the small particles, and will also attract others which seek more substantial food items in the clouded water.

An equally important function of groundbaiting, however, is to accustom the fish to feeding on items of similar size or nature to that which is on the hook, and in much fishing the fine crumb mixture is used merely as a carrier for the samples of hookbait which are mixed into it. It is thus possible to throw them to a greater distance, more accurately and in closer concentration, or by using a heavy groundbait mixture, to carry them down to the bed before they are distributed. The feeding habits of the species, and the type of water being fished, are obviously vital factors to consider in deciding the pattern of groundbaiting.

Important though it sometimes is, groundbaiting is no substitute for a wise choice of the fishing spot. It may put fish in feeding mood by showing them many food items, and it may encourage them to concentrate their attention on the

Drifting groundbait attracts and concentrates fish

type of food which is offered, but it will not attract fish into conditions which do not otherwise suit their tastes.

A finely ground cereal groundbait may be perfectly adequate for a great deal of fishing if it is properly used, but there are times when it will need supplementing before it will do what is required.

In a powerful current the standard mixture, even if thrown well upstream, would be broken up and swept away before reaching the bed, passing high above most worthwhile fish. If mashed potato is worked into it a more solid, binding mixture will result which will sink faster and break up much less readily.

In still waters and slow flowing canals an important part of groundbaiting is the cloud hanging in the water into which bait samples are scattered sparingly but frequently. A long-lasting cloud is obtained if a little milk powder is mixed into a fine crumb base.

A similar aim lies behind the use of fine leaf mould and loam, damped to bind together for throwing, into which bait

Groundbait sets fish searching for tit-bits

samples, very often bloodworms, are mixed. This method is locally popular in the canals of the North of England and in some Dutch waters.

Tench are often brought into feeding mood by the creation of mud clouds such as they themselves stir up when foraging in the bottom silt. Mud, sand and ground clay can achieve this attractive condition when it is not possible to rake the bed.

Tench, and some other species less noticeably, are undoubtedly attracted by the scent of blood in a groundbait. Oxblood, easily obtained from an abbatoir, should be allowed to congeal and then be worked into a bread and bran mixture.

There is much fishing where the most effective groundbaiting involves the use of bait samples only. This is generally so when the bait is a fairly large item such as a lobworm, a minnow, a piece of sausage, etc. A very few samples, introduced frequently so that there are some always present in the vicinity of the hookbait, will go a long way towards ensuring that the fish will be willing to accept the one with the hook in it.

Bait samples enclosed in containers to ensure concentration

It is necessary sometimes to use special methods to ensure that the groundbait reaches the right place in the right manner.

When fishing for bottom-feeding species in deep and fast water, for example, it is necessary to get the groundbait down to the bed before it breaks up and releases the samples of bait. This can be done by enclosing it within a tightly closed and weighted paper bag or the more recently available soluble bag.

By tradition, worms are enclosed within a ball of clay, a method still very effective.

Also available is a pre-shaped soluble cup, itself composed of a compressed groundbait compound, into which bait items can be packed to disperse on the bed as the container disintegrates.

It is frequently desirable to introduce bait samples continually though lightly over a long period, for it is generally true that a long period of feeding brings a long period of benefit.

Few anglers will be able to follow the traditional advice to hang the carcase of a sheep over the stream to drip maggots for many weeks, but a perforated tin of maggots, replenished as needed, will achieve the same result.

A net or loosely woven sack of broken bread can be anchored on fast water to send fragments down the current over a long period, a method which is very effective with chub and especially useful where the current swings in to run alongside a vertical bank.

Fast shallows above a deeper run offer the chance to place a large pile of groundbait so that an inch or two of water is constantly eroding the base of the pile to maintain a steady stream of particles downstream.

Although it may not be strictly defined as groundbaiting many outlets from drains, food processing plants, etc, act in the same way in concentrating fish in the area and accustoming them to feeding there. One can, with advantage, be alert for such features.

Drip feeding of maggots. Compressed bait container

Groundbaiting Devices

The swim-feeder is a device designed to be affixed permanently to the line whilst fishing, as a legering weight. Its hollow interior is packed with groundbait and bait samples which are washed out by the current to roll very accurately around the bait. It is commonly used where maggot baits are used for bottom-feeding fish in a flow of some power.

The bait dropper is used either by attaching it temporarily to the line or by having another rod made up for the purpose. This device is swung out to the fishing spot and allowed to sink to the bed, its contents being released mechanically as it touches.

A method of throwing small bait samples to a long distance has a largely localised popularity in the North of England. This is the throwing stick, usually a length of large diameter bamboo with one end plugged to give a suitable recess for holding maggots, chrysalids, hemp, etc., which can be thrown to a small area at a considerable distance.

Swim feeders and bait droppers give precise placing

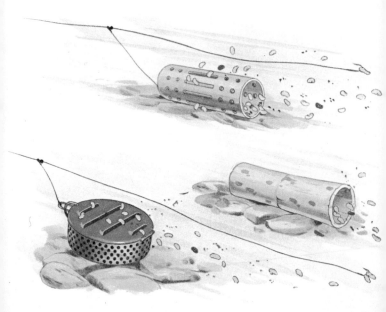

Methods of placing groundbait at long distance

The same purpose is served by using a catapult whose pouch will contain small baits which cannot easily be thrown by hand.

Some situations call for a little ingenuity in devising methods of groundbaiting. Very large lakes, where the fishing is at a great distance, can call for groundbaiting at a distance far greater than can be thrown by hand. A stiff mixture, moulded around the end of a flexible stick several feet long, can be thrown with accuracy to an astonishing range.

A less vigorous method, for use when the wind is convenient, is to float out a load of groundbait on a raft, with a line attached to a short mast. When the desired position is reached, a pull on the line will tip the raft and deposit the load. If a weak link is set into the end of the line, a sharp tug will break it, when the line can be reeled in and the raft recovered from the opposite bank later.

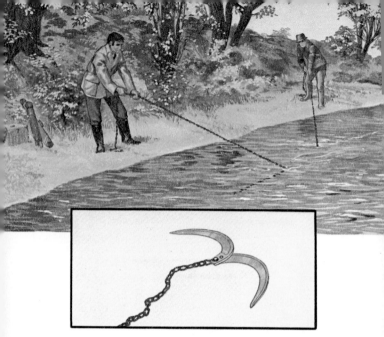

Clearing a pitch in heavily weeded water

Preparing a Still-water Swim

Those still waters which produce large stocks of good fish usually produce prolific plant growths too, and it is sometimes necessary to remove some of the weed in order to be able to catch the fish. It must be remembered, though, that because they give shelter and refuge, and are hosts to many of the organisms upon which the fish feed, the plants provide the reason for the presence of the fish. Weed clearing, therefore, should be restricted to the minimum necessary for effective fishing to take place.

A length of thin chain, weighted to hold bottom and drawn by two operators spaced some yards apart, will remove all but the toughest of bottom rooted weed. Single handed clearing can be done quite quickly by throwing out and retrieving a drag made by rivetting together two sickle blades.

Tench in particular, being much given to rooting in bottom

silt for food items, usually respond well to a vigorous raking of the bed which clouds the water and releases larvae, etc., bait samples being scattered into the cloud. If food items are scattered before raking, some will be buried and will occupy the attention of the tench for a longer period.

All bottom feeding species will move into a raked swim and will feed there both on the natural food items and on the angler's samples. Bream and roach are often caught in large numbers following this preparation, and carp are commonly attracted also.

Where weed growth is slight or is interspersed with open spaces, the weed is best left undisturbed except for ensuring that there is a clear channel for bringing fish to the bank.

Swim preparation in these circumstances is best confined to feeding only, the main feeding area being in open water adjacent to weed growth but extending in radiating lines out into the weeds as as to direct fish into the spot where it is planned to fish. Two or three weeks is not too long to maintain the food supply before fishing commences.

Prolific plant growth usually points to good fish

Float Fishing

To a great many anglers all fishing is float fishing and most anglers find a mesmeric pleasure in watching a float even though its indications may be entirely negative.

Fascinating though it may be to watch a float however, the method should be chosen to suit the conditions and the species and not be a matter of mere habit.

Often enough one consideration alone will decide the matter: the amount of weight needed to present the bait in the way desired. This will determine the type of float, the fishing depth, the distance one can cast, and so on, and the method will then have chosen itself.

It is necessary to have in mind the feeding habits of the species likely to be encountered, the depth at which they are likely to feed, the type of water they most favour, and to take note of the light intensity, water temperature, and any local factors which influence the location and behaviour of the fish.

Groundbaiting whilst fishing may bring about a change in the way the fish behave, perhaps causing them to take a higher position in the water as they intercept food items drifting down to them, perhaps concentrating some of them in slacks and eddies where food items tend to accumulate. Adjustments to the float, in its depth, shotting, type, may thus have to be made quite frequently whilst fishing is in progress.

It is generally true that the largest fish feed in a slower and more deliberate style and are likely more often to fall for baits which are fished stationary on the bed. To some extent, therefore, the depth and shotting of the float can decide whether a few large fish are caught or more numerous smaller ones.

It is worth reflecting on the fact that quite frequently fish are caught by only one of a number of anglers fishing very close together. At least sometimes this occurs because of a small, apparently insignificant difference in the presentation of the bait. This should encourage very thoughtful consideration before one settles for a particular style.

The float must suit the style and the conditions

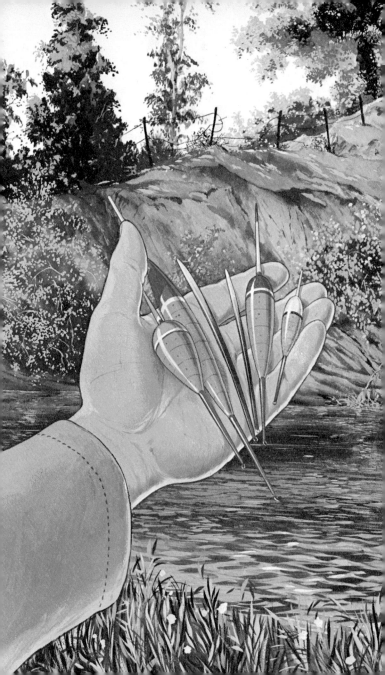

Swimming the Stream

This very active style of float fishing presents the bait in flowing water so that it travels down the current as nearly as possible as do the loose items which are usually thrown into the swim whilst fishing.

This style is invariably used with fine line, a small bait, such as maggot, chrysalids, etc., on a small hook, with a small, delicately shotted float which will respond decisively to bites.

This tackle is clearly inadequate to deal comfortably with the more powerful species, but it is best to make no concession to their possibility but to regard this style as especially suitable for roach, dace, small bream, shoal chub, etc., the fish which can be closely concentrated by groundbaiting into a fairly short swim where they can be caught at close range.

Traditionally, one sits centrally in the chosen length, casting two or three rod lengths upstream and lifting the rod to keep close contact with the float and be able to strike sharply.

The path of the tackle when swimming the stream

Swimming the stream - ready to retrieve

As the float passes the angler the rod is lowered to feed out the line and allow further travel of the bait. It is important not to pull the float during the first half of its travel nor to hold it back unduly during the second, but to leave the bait free all the time to respond to the minor sub-currents and eddies as would a loose item.

Normally the float is set so that the bait just trips along the bed, and loose feed is thrown far enough upstream to have sunk to the same depth by the time it passes through the swim. Failure on this point can spread the fish vertically through the water and make a large catch unlikely.

With modern reels and lines the method can be extended by casting further upstream and allowing longer travel below the angler. In this case, line must be retrieved on to the reel as the float approaches the angler and fed out again as it travels away from him.

At the end of the swim the float should be held back briefly to lift the bait in the water. This point often brings a fish which has been picking up stray items and also allows the tackle to swing into the bank before recovery so that the swim is not disturbed as one retrieves prior to a fresh cast.

Long Trotting

The essence of this style is that the float is allowed to draw line from the reel, either a free-running centre pin or a fixed spool reel with the pick-up open, as it travels down the current. It is suited to long stretches of open water where the current is moderate and the bed fairly level, and can be used in some rivers only when frost has cleared weeds.

The tackle needs to be somewhat specialised to function properly. A long rod, from 12 feet upwards, gives far better control of the tackle and of fish at range which may extend to forty yards or more.

A substantial float is essential, both to draw line from the reel and to carry enough weight to ensure that the bait is held down in the water. The body of the float should have deep vertical flutings to give a grip on the water so that the line can be straightened without disturbing the path of the tackle.

The long rod also permits the long, sweeping strike which is necessary to pick up a long line, take up the slack and stretch,

Long trotting in progress

Straightening the line in long trotting

and deliver an effective strike at ranges up to the limit of float visibility.

The line will usually need to be in the range 3–5 lb., with a hook size between 12 and 6, for the roach, dace, chub, grayling usually taken by this method, but both could well be a little stronger where large chub are a possibility and the current is powerful.

To fish finer is to invite trouble. It takes a long time to bring even a modest fish from the end of a long run, and small, fine hooks have time to cut through their fragile hold.

In general, baits for this method can well be larger than usual, flake, paste, cheese, etc., in generous portions, lob-worms, large bunches of maggots, all offering a good mouthful.

Groundbait is useful if the current will take it where it is needed, and samples of the hook bait should be sent down the current from time to time.

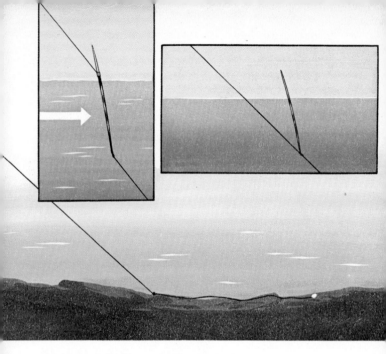

Laying on in flowing and still water

Laying on, float legering and stret pegging

Laying on is a style of stationary float fishing useful in both lakes and rivers, in which the weight, which is fixed on the line, and the bait, are lying on the bed. The distance from float to weight is set a little greater than the water depth so that the float is half-cocked by tightening the line and will respond to a bite whether it tightens or slackens the line.

A long, slim quill float is ideal, fixed at top and bottom for use in a current, fixed at the lower end only in still water. The weight should be kept as light as will hold position.

The normal way of fishing this style in running water is to make the cast across and down the current, allowing the tackle then to find its own resting place in a slightly gentler current. This goes far towards ensuring that the bait comes to rest in a place where loose items can be expected to be deposited by the current. It can, however, be fished in the opposite direction, casting up the current, though in this case the float will need to be set considerably deeper than the water.

Float legering is exactly the same as laying on except that the weight, a drilled bullet, a swivelled 'bomb', or a string of shot on a nylon link, is free to slide on the line. In theory this means that a fish can draw line without moving or feeling the lead: in practice the lead remains still only if it is appreciably heavier than it otherwise needs to be. There is little point in distinguishing between the two methods since they operate identically.

These methods ensure that the bait is being presented stationary on the bed, that fish will find it as they search for items which have come to rest behind stones, in depressions, beneath weed strands, etc.

Stret pegging is a traditional river style in which the tackle is cast directly down current from the rod tip with the float set over-depth, so that the weight and bait find bottom downstream of a half-cocked float. After a suitable interval, the rod is lifted a little and a little line fed out, to allow the tackle to resume its position slightly further downstream. Repetition of this process allows a very thorough search of the bed downstream of the fishing position.

Stret-pegging, a fine river style

The 'lift' method, with line sunk to combat wind

The lift method

This method of presenting a stationary bait on the bottom is exclusively a style for still waters. In its simplest form, which is adequate for a great deal of fishing for roach, tench and bream, one swan shot is used to cock a short length of peacock quill, which is fixed by the lower end only and is set at exactly water depth. Adjustment to the balance between float and weight are best made by snipping bits from the quill.

The rod must be set on a rest, for with the tackle properly adjusted, the slightest movement of the rod will cause violent movement at the float. Wind will affect this rig also; it is necessary then to sink the rod tip and the line below the surface.

Baits of paste, flake, bunches of maggots, should be set no more than two inches from the weight so that on picking up a bait the fish must lift the slot too. The float will then pop up sharply, an indication which calls for an immediate strike.

Lobworm baits are better set about a foot from the weight so there is time for the bait to be taken wholly into the fish's mouth before the weight is moved.

This method has been refined to cater for suspicious and shy-biting fish such as large roach. For this a special design of float is needed, having a buoyancy bob low down the stem and a long antenna of small diameter.

A shot is placed below the float sufficient to submerge the float to the point at which one tiny dust shot added near to the bait will leave the required length of antenna emergent.

The benefit of this rig is that the fish has an irreducible amount of weight to lift, such as is unlikely to cause dropping of the bait, and due to the small volume of the antenna, the lifting of this tiny weight causes a relatively large float movement.

On first using this method most anglers find it a little difficult to react quickly to bites whose indication comes in the opposite direction to what is usual, but this is a most effective and valuable style for still waters.

The lift method in action

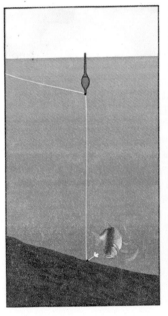 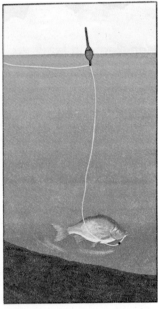

A selection of leger weights

Legering and leger weights

The last few decades have seen enormous development of legering techniques, but there are still some anglers who regard it as a rather lazy method to which they may resort when float fishing has failed. They are quite wrong.

The term legering embraces so many variations and refinements that it might well be maintained to be the most versatile of angling methods, capable of coping at least as well as any other method with almost every circumstance and species.

Legering is certainly infinitely adaptable, and having studied the place being fished, its distance, depth, current, the possible fishing positions, the probable species, the way in which one wishes the bait to come to the fish, one can always select, adapt or devise a legering method to meet the needs of the situation.

The weight is an important component of successful legering and time is well spent in ensuring that it is exactly right and of the right type for a particular job.

By far the most versatile weight is a string of shot nipped on to a short length of nylon folded over the line. This is readily and delicately adjustable, less prone to snagging than most and more readily released when caught up.

Much legering can be done perfectly well, both in rivers and still waters, with no more than one or two shot nipped direct on to the reel line.

The streamlined, swivelled bomb is extremely popular and effective for general use in a wide range of sizes and is unbeatable for very long range casting.

There are several designs of pyramid and flattened leads, some swivelled, some drilled, which will hold to the bottom in very fast currents.

The old favourite, the drilled bullet, is a good weight for rolling down the current provided the bed is clear and even.

For static legering in still water where there is a depth of bottom weed or soft silt, the weight can usefully have a stem of a length to hold the line clear.

In all legering it must be remembered that the weight is by far the commonest cause of dropped baits and alarmed fish. It should always be as small as possible and dispensed with entirely whenever possible.

A pyramid lead, paternoster style, holds fast in currents

The Rolling Leger

This style of angling enables the angler to search for his fish, covering his swim foot by foot with the bait always on or very near to the bed.

The amount of weight is crucial to correct operation. It needs to be such that it just fails to hold bottom securely, but is rolled down the current a little at a time, holding briefly here and there, as the current on the submerged line varies.

The shot link weight is best for this style as it is so easily and delicately adjustable, though a swivelled bomb weight is very suitable provided its weight is right for the conditions.

The usual practise is to cast across, or down and across, the current and feel for contact with the weight with the rod held high. If the weight fails to roll the rod should be lowered so as to submerge more line and thus increase the pull of the current. Eventually the tackle will have travelled in an arc which ends almost directly downstream of the angler, at which point it is retrieved and cast to a slightly different starting position.

While a cast is being fished out the angler should be holding the line lightly between finger and thumb, at the same time watching the rod tip and the bow of line falling from it. He will thus both see and feel a bite, ensuring the earliest possible indication.

There will, of course, be times when obstructions on the bank or in the water will compel some modification of the basic style, perhaps by restricting the arc of the bait's travel, perhaps preventing the approach being made from the head of the swim. There is no reason why a rolling leger should not initially be cast upstream, with line being retrieved to keep in touch with the weight as it returns towards the angler.

Legering should never become a stereotyped method, but regarded as adaptable to whatever conditions and circumstances one encounters.

The rolling leger is an effective method to use when roving a stretch of river, searching for fish, or when giving thorough coverage to a chosen swim.

The rolling leger in action

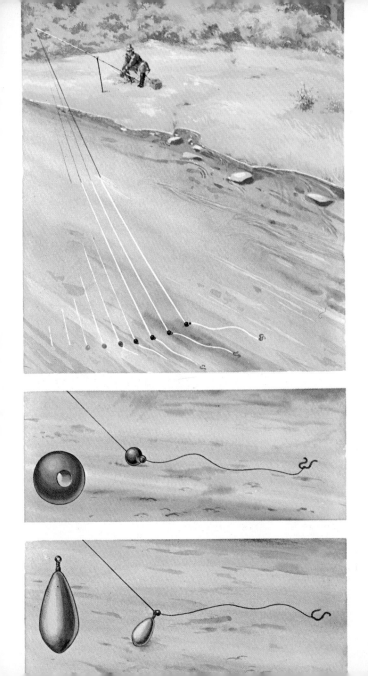

The trail

The trail refers to that part of the line between the weight and the hook, the distance within which the bait is free to respond to the influences of the water, and the distance which a fish could possibly move the bait without signalling a bite.

The length of the trail can be a vital factor and there are several considerations which govern its choice. In all forms of legering, static or rolling, which are used in running water, it must be remembered that a long trail allows the bait to respond to water movement more nearly as does a loose item, resting in the slightly slacker spots behind stones, under weed, in hollows, the places where fish might be accustomed to finding food items deposited by the current. There are circumstances in which a trail of five or six feet would not be too long.

A long trail allows the cast to be made into an area of clear bed where the weight can rest while the bait can roll down

A long trail allows the bait to fall slowly near the bed, a short trail gives early indication of bites

below weed growth. Similarly, a cast can be made upstream of an overhead obstruction such as trailing branches, allowing a bait on a long trail to be carried down into the sheltered swim below.

In both still and running water a bait on a long trail will sink more slowly after the weight has found bottom, giving the double advantage that the bait is pulled quickly through the surface shoals of small fish and then falls freely and enticingly for the last few feet, where the larger fish usually are.

A short trail is called for, as little as one or two inches, to anchor a buoyant bait such as crust just above the bottom where it is easily seen as the current gives it an attractive wavering.

A fragile bait or one easily sucked from the hook should be used on a short trail so as to obtain the earliest possible indication of a fish touching the bait, and for the same reason a short trail should be used when fish are biting shyly or tentatively.

The length of the trail, though, should not be a matter of

Upstream legering with line as indicator

habit or of hard-and-fast rules, but a matter for experiment in the light of conditions at the time of fishing and of the mood of the fish. At some times it is a matter of no importance at all, at others it is crucial.

Upstream Legering

There are places on most rivers where the easiest approach is from the downstream end of a swim. Far from being a problem, this approach can give significant advantages over other styles of legering.

The weight needed, whether it is to hold the bait stationary or allow it to roll, is considerably less than when fishing downstream, which means that biting fish are much less likely to feel its drag and eject the bait.

The angler is casting from behind his fish which means that at close range or in shallow water he is much less likely to scare them before they have had a chance to take his bait.

Hooked fish will be played with the current in the angler's favour, making it possible to draw them more quickly away from the shoal and to continue to bring them smoothly down the stream even should they get into weed.

There are two distinct ways of achieving a delicately balanced rig. The first is to use the lightest possible weight which when cast upstream and allowed to find botton will just hold its position, with the line falling in a slack curve from the high-pointing rod. To attempt to straighten the line should be enough to dislodge the weight.

The slight pull of a bite will also be enough to cause the weight to roll down the current a little, upon which the already slack line will be seen to fall yet slacker. A long, sweeping strike will be needed to straighten the slack line and reach the fish.

The second method is more suited to windy conditions when it would be difficult to watch a slack line. The weight is deliberately more than is strictly needed so that having made the cast and put the rod on a rest, angled upwards, the line can be tightened against the weight almost to the point of dislodging it, and enough slightly to flex the rod tip.

The pull of a bite, added to that of the current and the taut line, will dislodge the precariously holding weight, the rod tip will be seen to straighten and the line to slacken.

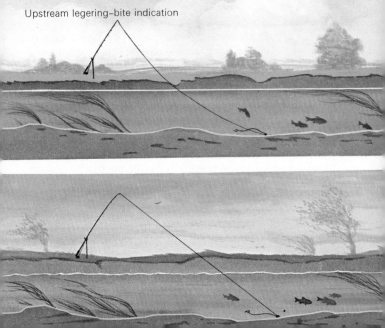

Upstream legering–bite indication

Detecting bites on leger tackle

Bite detection on leger tackle

Inventive anglers are constantly striving to devise new means of detecting bites on leger tackle and one can choose from a wide range of gadgetry involving pivoted arms, levers, springs, luminous and audible alarms, and a host of more homely methods.

There is no doubt, though, that for a great deal of fishing there is no gadget to beat the fingers of a well-practised angler holding the line while he watches the rod tip or the line beyond it.

Some devices, however, achieve a wide popularity and are undoubtedly effective. One such is the swing tip, which acts as a hinged extension to the rod, variable for weight according to the current, which lifts or falls on a bite. This is widely used for bream fishing, particularly in wide rivers, and for general bottom fishing in both still and running waters.

The traditional dough bobbin, a bit of paste pinched on to

the line at any point along or beyond the rod, is a reliable and simple means of making bites visible in all but strong winds.

Gaining some popularity for use when bites are small and delicate, as is quite often the case with roach, is the quiver tip, a rod tip extension which is very flexible, so as to make for visible movement with very little drag.

Drag, i.e. resistance felt by a biting fish, is the factor which decides how quick must be the angler's reaction. When bites are being missed because fish are quickly ejecting the bait, the remedy is not to strive desperately to strike more quickly, but to rearrange the system of bite indication so that the fish feels less drag, and it should always be borne in mind that only when the fish has nothing to move but a length of line has minimum drag been achieved.

In situations where the reel pick-up can be left open as widely spaced bites are awaited, there is much to be said for a slip of metal foil folded on the line. This, virtually weightless, causes no significant drag and its movement as line is drawn is not only visible but clearly audible also.

The swing tip, a popular bite indicator for legering

Spinning with artificial lures

Lures, like floats, have an attraction of their own, quite apart from their effectiveness in catching fish, and the do-it-yourself angler finds in them a great scope for experiment.

There are instances of artificial lures tempting almost every species of fish and it is possible that if wider experiment was made the scope of lure fishing could be much extended. Meanwhile the method is virtually confined to the pursuit of pike, perch, to a lesser extent chub, and to the basses.

Basically, lures fall into two groups, those which by their appearance seek to resemble, when in action, a fish or other item of natural diet, and those which by their colour, flash, and action seek merely to act as attractors. Some lures include elements of both groups, having a flashy, spinning part in front of a very realistic fish body.

Traditional designs such as spoons, devons, wagtails, etc. still catch their share of fish, but developments, mainly originating in the U.S.A., where lure fishing figures more largely in the

Types of spoon lures, traditional but still effective

angling scene, are now appearing more commonly in Europe. Plugs are available in many designs, sizes, colours, materials and finishes to work fussily along the surface, to run just submerged and to work deeply.

Jigs, weighted to suit all conditions, are gaining popularity more slowly but their use is spreading.

Exactly why a fish, which can be assumed to have good under-water vision and sensory equipment to identify water-transmitted vibrations, should attack blatantly unnatural objects may be a little puzzling, but it is a fact that the best of lures are invariably those whose working can be felt through the rod, and it seems likely that the vibrations caused by the lure are more important in attracting fish than is the appearance.

Certainly, so far as the purely predatory species are concerned, the important thing in lure fishing is to ensure, by choice of lure and by the way in which the tackle is manipulated, that it moves through the water with marked movement, vibrating, spinning, wobbling, for it is the movement which draws the fish to it.

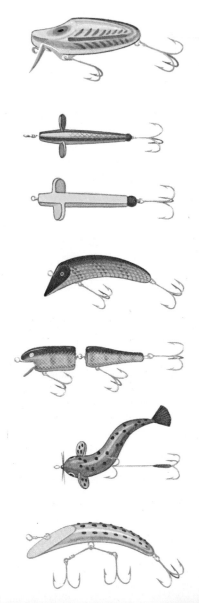

Plugs and devon minnows, useful for all predators

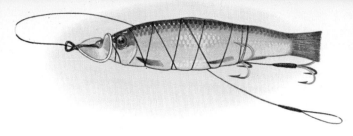

Natural baits mounted for spinning

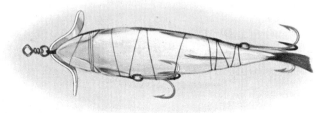

Spinning with natural baits

The term 'spinning', though commonly used in this context, is not really appropriate since very few anglers today mount their natural baits with spinning vanes or fins, and though baits so mounted must have caught very many fish during the centuries that this method has endured, it is now accepted as sensible to make a natural bait behave in a more natural manner.

Baits for pike depend to some extent on the size of fish one expects to catch, though fish as small as sprats will sometimes attract very large pike. Almost every species of fish has been successfully used as bait, but the most commonly used is probably a roach of about four ounces.

The trace is threaded through the bait from vent to mouth so as to draw a treble hook up to the vent. A bead or button on the trace above the hook will make the bait less liable to tearing during casting. The lips of the bait should be bound together around the trace to make the bait more durable in fishing, and if long casting is anticipated an additional large single hook should be inserted downwards into the head of the bait to share the strain.

A bait so mounted will sink fairly slowly and time must be allowed after casting for it to approach the bed. A lift of the rod, upon which a little line is retrieved, will bring it curving up again, sometimes to break the surface, when it is allowed once again to dive and spiral its way back into the depths. It thus travels back towards the angler in a series of vertical zig-zags.

For searching very deep waters a drilled bullet or similar weight can be slipped on the trace and pushed down the throat of the bait. For surface fishing, sometimes very effective in summer when weed is thick, the bait can be stuffed with expanded polystyrene so as to float high in the water, and worked along with a good splashy action.

Spinning with natural baits for perch and other relatively small species takes much the same form as for pike, except that the baits will range from minnow size to that of gudgeon, and the tackle strength modified to suit the quarry. Lines of 8–10 lb. breaking strain are needed for pike, half that strength would be adequate for perch, etc.

Perch respond best to a bait which is retrieved fairly slowly, with short, sharp spurts every few yards. If a perch is seen to follow the bait, it should be drawn away rapidly to spur an attack.

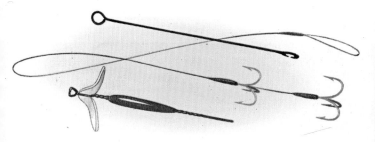

Spinning flights

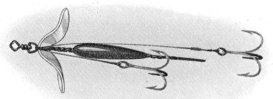

Fly fishing

There is little doubt that if one wished to prove the point it would be possible to catch every species of fish by some style of fly fishing.

Perch are caught freely on the wet flies of trout anglers, especially when the fly is a flashy attractor or a fish imitation such as the Polystickle or Muddler Minnow. The basses too are good takers of flies.

Roach eat many nymphs and larvae in their natural diet and are readily caught on imitations, particularly the roach of small, clear streams. Floating flies occasionally appeal to roach, and an imitation shrimp or caddis larva appeals to roach and most other small species.

Barbel are caught on deeply-fished weighted flies on the Continent and no doubt could be elsewhere by anyone willing to spend enough time in experiments to find the tackle, style and fly patterns needed.

The fact that pike can be caught on flies has been demonstrated very conclusively by anglers with sheer fun in mind, using heavy trout tackle and reservoir rods. Salmon fly

Fly fishing will take all kinds of fish

tackle would cope very well with even very large pike. Flies for pike should be long streamers tied on large single hooks, or tube flies, both dressed with plenty of feather so as to give a good movement in the water.

Grayling of course, are such good takers of a fly that they are frequently cursed by trout anglers who take them unintentionally. This is pure prejudice, for grayling fight doggedly and make a meal equal to trout.

Shoaling dace in fast water will take a small fly eagerly and with a speed which will test the reaction of the most expert fly fisherman. Occasionally they are more discriminating and one must match a natural fly on the water.

Chub are traditionally lovers of a large well-hackled fly floated beneath overgrown banks, trailing branches and the like on still summer days. Small shoal chub will compete for almost any fly, wet or dry, and a large imitation of a moth will take chub well when they have moved into shallow water after dusk.

Rudd are splendid takers of a fly during the summer months and as they are usually in large shoals heavy bags can be taken. A green or brown nymph, fished slowly in very small pulls just sub-surface will take rudd with near certainty.

The barbel, a handsome and powerful fish

SPECIES

The Barbel (*Barbus barbus*)

The barbel is a superb sporting fish, much esteemed by anglers for its great power and considerable size. It is widely distributed throughout Europe with fish of between ten and fifteen pounds not uncommon. It is a relative of the Indian Mahseer (*Barbus putitoria*) which may reach a length of 8 feet, and of several African species which achieve weights approaching 40 pounds.

Distribution in British waters is restricted to the Rivers Thames, Avon, Stour, Kennet, Severn and the Yorkshire river system, though colonies are becoming established elsewhere following stocking programmes.

Barbel are omnivorous with a diet including small fish, crustacea, larvae, soft weed, crayfish, lampreys, etc., and they rapidly become accustomed to the commonly used baits.

As the beautifully shaped body shows, the barbel is essentially a bottom feeding fish, liking fast, smooth runs, especially where these exist between beds of weed. Here they will often lie for much of the day, especially during bright weather, hidden under the weed except when waving fronds expose them briefly or when they drop down to the tail of the weed to pick up a passing food item.

In parts of some barbel fisheries careful observation allows one to pin-point individual fish or small groups and to fish specifically for them. Where the water is deep or coloured one has to look for suitable water conditions and fish hopefully.

At all times, but especially early in the year, barbel haunt the fast water of weir pools and the like, sometimes right up in the fast water, sometimes in glassy fast glides down the sides of the pool.

Although basically a fish of the faster water, barbel do nevertheless sometimes move into slack areas with silty beds. This happens commonly on well-fished rivers where ground-baiting and loose feeding provide many particles to be deposited by the current in the quiet areas, often quite close to the bank. Here the barbel come to feed after sunset, and on many waters this is the most favourable time and situation.

Barbel often feed well through the dark hours during the warmer months, sometimes, in spite of their underslung mouths, right at the surface in weed beds.

The power of the barbel, and the fast, weedy water in which it is often found, call for more powerful tackle than that suitable for general fishing. The rod should be of 10–12

A small selection of baits for barbel

feet, with a full action, used with a line of between 5 and 10 lb. breaking strain, according to the water conditions and the run of fish expected. Hooks should be as large as can be properly used, depending on the nature and size of the bait, ranging from size 4 to size 12.

Barbel are caught on a very wide range of baits including the bread baits, maggots, worms, minnows, cheese, sausage, meats, seeds and grains. In some waters a popular bait is used almost exclusively, inducing a high degree of pre-occupation, and there is little prospect of success with any bait unless a feeding programme is first carried out.

By far the most widely used method is legering, either to present a static bait in a favourable spot or to search an area with rolling tackle. The type of weight will depend on the method, and the power of the current, but should always be kept as little as possible.

Barbel water : good flow, healthy weed growth, clean bed

When using maggots and similar small baits the bait dropper and the swim feeder are used as an adjunct to legering to ensure a steady supply of bait samples right on the bottom exactly downstream of the bait.

Suitable swims, of even depth and clean bed, can be fished effectively by long trotting. The float needs to be very substantial carrying enough weight to keep the bait tripping along the bed.

Laying on with float tackle is an effective way of fishing slacker areas identified as feeding grounds. The float should be set at a depth a little greater than the water and allowed to drift into a settled position.

After dark, smooth glides close to the bank offer the best prospects for legering, at which time large meaty baits are usually the most successful.

Barbel are occasionally caught, usually by accident, during the late part of the season, but they are essentially a fish of the summer and autumn months.

Above: silver bream.   Below: common bream

Common Bream (*Abramis brama*) and
Silver Bream (*Blicca bjoernka*)

One of the most widely distributed of European fishes the common or bronze bream flourishes in almost every river system and in numberless lakes, canals, reservoirs, etc. The silver bream is much less common, is rarely fished for specifically and is usually of an insignificant size.

Outstanding amongst British bream waters are the Broads and rivers of Norfolk and the Fens, though many other waters hold large stocks of sizeable fish. The Irish central plain, a limestone area including parts of Eire and Northern Ireland, offers bream fishing of the highest quality in its many rivers and loughs, with immense shoals of fish of high average weight.

Bream are commonly caught at weights up to about 5 lb. with occasional specimens approaching double that weight. Most large shoals, however, consist of fish in the range 1–4 lb.

In general river bream favour the steadier currents, though exceptionally they are found in quite fast water. Invariably they are concentrated in dense shoals which move around as they feed, and heavy groundbaiting is needed to hold a shoal.

Bream live and feed largely on the bottom, though occasionally they show themselves by swirling or rolling at the surface. Otherwise shoals can often be located by the appearance of extensive mud stains, sometimes with patches of bubbles rising, caused by the activity of fish feeding in the bottom silt.

Although remaining active throughout the year, the summer feeding is most greedy and at this time it is almost impossible to use too much groundbait.

Bream are often active feeders by night, usually with the heaviest feeding concentrated into the early hours of darkness and around dawn. A still, warm, cloudy night is a good time to take a heavy bag in a well prepared swim.

Most baits will take bream, though it is sometimes necessary to experiment a good deal to find the right one for the day. Worms are usually good, so are maggots and all kinds of bread baits.

Most bream fishing is in quiet currents

Very large bream present a challenge to the angler, for even when located they are usually very difficult to tempt. It is probable that like very large fish of most species they are partly piscivorous.

In still waters where it is not necessary to fish at long range, and in slow currents which are not of great depth, float fishing is often the most effective and pleasant way of taking bream.

It may be that a bait which is rolling along the bed will attract more bites, in which case the lowest shot should be set to clear the bed leaving enough trail to allow the bait to respond to the influence of the flow. More usually, though, the shoal would have been concentrated by groundbaiting, with the bait being taken more readily if it is presented stationary on the bottom by ordinary laying on methods.

When bream are feeding eagerly their bites show characteristically as a preliminary lift or tilt of the float followed by a

Bream are largely bottom feeders

Heavy bags of bream can be taken at night

slow, sliding away. The strike can safely be delayed until the float is clearly drawn away.

Float legering, involving, as it does, the use of a greater weight, is useful for casting float tackle to a greater range. This is a good method for the bream of larger lakes and reservoirs where bream may rarely be found in the shelving margins. Where deep water and a long range have both to be contended with a sliding float is best used with this method.

Though the bream is perhaps not one of the most sensitive species, float tackle for all styles should be chosen to offer the least possible drag to a biting fish, or dropped baits will inevitably be a problem.

Night fishing for bream, using float tackle, has an atmosphere all its own. Normal laying on or float legering can be used, depending on the range, in conjunction with a light shining on the float. The lamp should throw a narrow beam and should be rigidly fixed low down to shine almost parallel with the surface of the water. No light will then penetrate the

Chequer board to aid bite detection

surface and the behaviour of the fish will in no way be affected. A yellow or white float tip will show very clearly in the light beam.

When bream have to be fished for at considerable range or in very deep water, and also where they are found in currents of considerable strength, legering methods come into their own.

The shot link weight is ideal, allowing ready adjustment to suit conditions and relative freedom from serious snagging.

The static style of still waters will suit slow reaches of wide rivers and will generally bring bites once the fish have been located or have been drawn to the chosen swim by groundbaiting. Bites can be detected by holding and watching the line, the strike being made before the fish has time to meet any significant resistance.

Satisfactory indication will also be given by any of the methods mentioned on pages 58–59, of which the current favourite is the swing tip, sometimes used in conjunction with a squared or chequered board against which small movements of the tip are more readily seen, and which shields the sensitive tip from wind.

River bream are much given to apparently random wandering in large shoals and when no sign of their presence can be seen a good deal of experimental fishing may be needed to find them. A more mobile approach is needed to do this economically.

A rolling leger tackle will offer the bait over a wide area of the bed at each cast, and, with a stride or two taken downstream between casts, allows a thorough coverage of a great deal of water in quite a short time.

Bream are rarely caught singly; if one fish comes there is usually a shoal waiting, and an accurate return to the same area, this time with a static rig, can be counted on to attract further fish. The supply of food in the form of groundbait must be kept up however, or it is likely that the shoal will soon continue its patrol.

Bites are rather unpredictable; sometimes a hearty pull is given, sometimes there is a mere twitch, sometimes a bite occurs while the bait is still falling. Thoughtful experiment with the length of trail will often provide a solution to difficult bites.

Bream are usually found in shoals

Crucian Carp (*Carassius carassius*) and Common Carp (*Cyprinus carpio*)

Although achieving no great size, the Crucian carp, thick-set, solid, and distinguished by its lack of barbules, is a sporting little fish, usually occuring at weights of 2–3 lb., whose shyness and delicacy of biting can test the skill of the angler. It is exclusively a fish of still waters, where it usually remains close to weed growth.

It is taken on a variety of baits, usually maggots, the bread baits and small worms, fished on fairly light float tackle.

The common carp has been introduced to many parts of the world, in some cases because it is locally much esteemed as a food fish, in others for its sporting possibilities. Over much of the continent of Europe it is a prized food fish, as it is in the Far East.

In Britain it is regarded as the aristocrat of the 'coarse' species, achieving a greater size than any other, and angled for with great dedication and specialisation.

In Australia, where it was introduced from Europe a century ago, it has thriven greatly, achieves a very large size,

The crucian carp, much smaller than the common carp

yet has little attraction as an anglers' fish and has, in some States, been officially classified as a pest and subjected to an eradication programme. In the United States carp are largely dismissed contemptuously as 'trash fish'.

More recently carp have been introduced to selected waters in Eire and Northern Ireland where the signs are that very large fish will result.

Most of the carp in British waters are of fast growing, hatchery-bred strains which show three variations: fully-scaled, known as common carp; partially scaled with outsize scales, known as mirror carp; and the scaleless form known as leather carp.

Much rarer is the so-called wild carp, a leaner, faster moving and very beautiful fish, very hard to tempt and very hard to land when tempted. 'Wild' carp do not often achieve weights above 8–10 lb., compared with the 40–60 lb. to which common carp will grow in most parts of the world.

Carp do exist in a few British rivers but rarely in numbers which warrant serious angling for them. The exceptions occur mostly where the warm outflow from electricity

The common carp, large, powerful, and very cautious

generating plants has in recent years brought a change in conditions, much to the taste of the carp.

It is to the lakes and gravel pits that the carp enthusiast looks for his sport, the most productive pools being those with a high proportion of shallow water and the richness of plant and animal life that goes with full penetration of light and warmth.

Early in the season carp will spend a good deal of their time deep within beds of soft weed feeding on the young growth, and often clearing large areas.

Until recent years carp were regarded as being exclusively a fish of the summer months, being in virtual hibernation by late Autumn, but persistent angling in defiance of tradition has proved that carp are catchable, at least in some waters, in temperatures almost down to freezing point, at all stages of the season.

A great deal of the carp's summer diet consists of organisms too small to be used as bait. When these occur in periodic

Carp can be observed in shallow margins

concentrations, as do the mud-living chironomid larvae and the free-swimming daphniae, the carp may become totally preoccupied with a single type and size of food and be virtually uncatchable.

At other times it is commonly found that extended periods of feeding are needed to accustom the carp to a particular type or size of food item which can then be used on the hook.

This process may have to be repeated at quite short intervals as the carp in some waters seem able rapidly to learn the dangers attaching to those types of food which have been most used.

The most consistently successful carp baits are bread, used as flake, paste, floating or submerged crust, or a balanced combination of paste and crust, parboiled potatoes, lobworms, large bunches of maggots, and freshwater mussels. They have been caught on very many others, even on artificial flies, and there is much scope for thoughtful experiment in the field of catching carp.

Surface feeding takes place notably during the warmer months and can be encouraged by scattering bits of bread

Floating crust, a very good summer bait for carp

crust over a lengthy period. Catching carp by surface fishing has a special tension and excitement as one can often watch the approach of the carp for some time before the eventual taking or rejection of the bait.

Breadcrust, at least half as large as a matchbox, on a hook no smaller than size 6, with a line in the range 6–10 lb., will be about right in most conditions. The crust, dipped in water to give weight, can be cast quite well, though it may be necessary to flick it out no further than the edge of marginal weeds.

No system of bite detection is needed. The bait should be left alone, allowed to drift in the breeze, or to lodge against surface-growing weed, exactly as would a loose item. Though carp sometimes make a considerable swirl when taking a bait from the surface they can also suck in a bait without a ripple showing. A keen watch should, therefore, be kept, on the hooked crust, or the carp may be away unnoticed.

In many pools, especially those which see a lot of angling, the carp often come close to the banks by night, clearing up floating scraps of groundbait, wind-blown fragments, etc., and these fish can be caught by a specialised form of surface fishing in which the bait is offered directly below the rod tip.

The ideal spot occurs where there is a depth of several feet right at the edge, and the ideal time comes when several days of warm breezes have blown onshore.

Powerful tackle is needed as the fish will be hooked on just a few feet of line right under the angler's feet. Line of 15 lb. breaking strain is not too heavy for large carp which have to be held hard right from the delivery of the strike.

The rod is set on rests with the crust bait just touching the water, the angler then remaining motionless and patient until a patrolling carp arrives on the scene. If small species are a nuisance the bait can be lifted to clear the surface, being lowered when swirling or sucking at the surface indicates the

Margin fishing at night, a very exciting method

presence of a carp. A few loose crusts in the area can serve as an attraction and an indication of feeding fish.

The nature of most bottom fishing for carp is dictated by two facts: that bites are invariably few and far between and that carp are extremely sensitive to any form of drag when they take the bait.

The normal style, both by day and by night, is to have nothing on the line but the baited hook, with the rod set on two rests, pointing at the bait. A fixed spool reel is used with the pick-up left open so that line can be drawn freely by a biting fish. The rod rests need to be of a type which does not impede the free passage of line.

Once the bait has been positioned the angler has only a waiting game to play, commonly for several hours, sometimes all day or all night. However long the wait, however, he should resist the temptation to move the bait for inspection or re-siting except very rarely.

Battery operated bite alarms, giving an audible signal, are very popular with carp anglers, especially by night, since they do not demand sustained concentration. Many other

Battery powered bite alarm, popular for carp fishing

drag-free systems of bite indication are quite suitable however.

Bites from carp frequently involve a long and fast run with the bait. The angler should ensure that line is running out smoothly before he engages the pick-up and strikes. At long ranges the strike must be hard and sweeping and may even need to be repeated.

All bites do not follow this pattern, though, some waters producing a high proportion of small, twitching pulls which are not so easy to time. It seems best some times to wait for a distinct run, however many twitches come first, at others it seems best to strike at the first little movement.

In most waters the night and the very early morning bring the best chance of carp, if only because these times are freer of disturbing influences, and the fish move more openly under cover of darkness.

In all carp fishing the tackle will be very thoroughly tested and it is folly to be ill-equipped. A very large landing net is essential.

The most important ingredient in successful carping, however, is the angler's caution and his patience, and his utter determination to catch carp.

Chub (*Leuciscus cephalus*)

This lovely, thick-set, brassy fish is to be found in almost all rivers, many small streams and a few still waters. One of its attractions for the angler is that in almost all waters at least some of the fish achieve a large size.

The finest chub fishing is found in clear rivers with a heavy growth of aquatic plants and prolific small organisms. In such waters chub of between 3 and 5 lb. are relatively plentiful.

Chub are extremely sensitive to disturbance of any kind, but especially to visible movement. To show a silhouette, unless fishing at very long range in a large river is to ensure failure as the chub exercise their peculiar talent for quietly fading away.

Immature chub retain the shoaling habit, but larger fish are usually found in small, loosely composed groups or as single fish occupying favoured spots.

By day chub do not usually stray far from weeds, often lying hidden beneath them when the light is bright, and are

The chub, a lover of weedy rivers

fond of the cover given by overhanging trees. Undercut or sheer banks are another favoured place where chub can often be found within a few inches of the bank and caught on baits which are merely lowered to them with extreme caution.

The range of waters in which chub will flourish shows their tolerance of widely differing conditions, and within the same fishery chub can be found in the rush of white water below a weir or fall, in smooth, glassy glides and in almost slack spots. The nearest one can come to a general rule is that during very hot weather the fast water offers the best prospects and in really cold conditions the chub are likely to drop back into quiet swims, even into slack back-waters. There are, however, plenty of exceptions even to this.

The chub is an unusually consistent feeder which is catchable from beginning to end of the season if you can find the right bait and presentation and pick the right spot, always provided you make sure the chub has no reason to suspect your presence.

The chub is probably the most completely omnivorous fish. It certainly eats every small aquatic creature shrimps, snails,

leeches, etc.; it takes larvae from the bed and flies from the surface; grubs, caterpillars, beetles, fruits and seeds are taken when they drop into the water; larger creatures are not safe from the chub's large mouth and powerful pharyngeal crushing teeth, and crayfish, frogs lampreys, etc., are taken along with any fish small enough to be engulfed.

In addition to its wide natural diet the chub is willing to try anglers' baits in great variety and it would be almost impossible to find a bait guaranteed to be immune from attack by chub.

Cheese is probably the most commonly-used bait, often mixed into soft bread paste, and it appears that the scent of cheese plays some part in its appeal. Bread is a good bait on most rivers, either as flake or crust.

Large lobworms are very good too, either fished singly or in bunches.

There seems to be a positive attraction in meaty baits,

Chub will accept almost any bait

especially those of a fatty nature, and sausage meat, luncheon meat, fat bacon, etc., are all effective baits for chub.

Wasp grubs provide another bait which appears to have a specific attraction for chub. These can be fished singly, in bunches, or if the chub are feeding really well, a chunk of comb containing grubs will be taken equally well. To get the best from this bait involves using groundbait into which comb and grubs have been mashed.

The smaller baits, such as maggots and wheat will take chub very well, especially if they are loose fed whilst fishing, but it should be remembered that if they attract small species too the catching of large chub becomes much less likely.

Where chub are concerned you can use as bait almost any item you fancy with a good chance that you will find a chub willing to sample it.

The majority of chub fishing is best done by a legering method, using a full actioned rod of 10–11 feet, a line of not

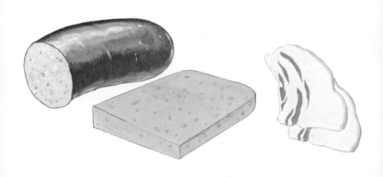

Some popular chub baits

less than 4 lb. breaking strain, and a hook of size 6–8. Where the weed growth is scattered or sparse, a rolling leger, fished down and across, is very effective.

Many of the best chub rivers are too rich in plant growth for this method, however, and fishing may then be confined to relatively small open areas into which a static leger tackle can be cast.

Static tackle can be used with a short trail to anchor the bait in the open ground or with a trail length which allows the bait to be carried down beneath the weeds, a spot often favoured by chub, especially in warm and bright conditions.

Alternatively, when chub are deep within weed beds, they can be fished for from the opposite direction, casting up-stream into the weed. This allows the tackle, and a hooked fish, to be brought through dense weed with ease and little danger of serious snagging.

Some of the spots which are likely to hold chub

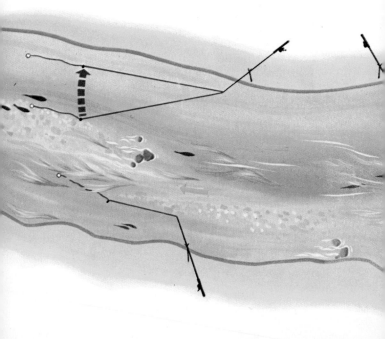

Lilies and similarly tough growths may equally well shelter the chub, but in this cast the bait should certainly be anchored in a clearing, for no fish is quicker than the chub to wrap the line around a root. A fish hooked near solid snags must be held very hard with no line yielded, and line strengths up to 8 lb. are called for where fish run to good weights.

It is sometimes possible to discover by observation or deduction a route over which patrolling chub pass regularly, and to place a bait there with the certainty that sooner or later a fish will arrive in the spot. It is sometimes worthwhile to scare away fish in putting the bait in position, with the knowledge that the eventual return is certain.

When winter brings low water temperatures the chub will usually be found in rather quieter stretches, and in intense cold they will fall back into almost slack water. They will still have brief periods of feeding, though, the best prospects being with a small bait presented stationary on the bed. Probably the best bait in these conditions is a small cube of crust tethered one or two inches above the bed.

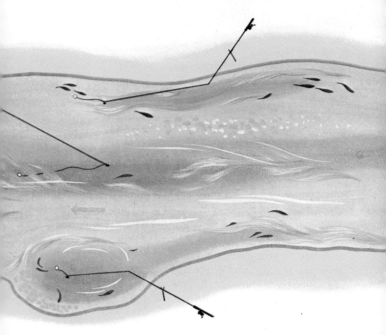

There are two circumstances when chub will probably respond best to float fishing. The first arises where a long run of open water permits float tackle to be trotted far down the current, covering a great deal of water from which fish may come at any point to the limit of visibility.

Judicious feeding of samples of the hook bait is valuable with this method, the feeding being sparing in winter, rather more generous in summer.

Chub love overhanging trees

The second circumstance arises in very cold conditions when fish have deserted the streamy water to lie quietly in almost slack water. The little feeding which takes place at this time is likely to be far less decisive than is usual with chub, and may be tentative and delicate. Light laying on will then give clearer indication of gentle bites on the small baits which are advisable in these conditions.

There is much to be said for using the simplest of tackle

whenever it is possible, a rod, a line and a hook, for each addition to the essentials is a potential source of alarm to the sensitive chub. This style, which has come to be known as free lining, can be used with many of the best chub baits – slugs, crayfish, small dead fish, bunches of lobworms, etc., which are substantial enough to be cast without additional weight.

There are few forms of angling more testing and fascinating

Chub can be expected alongside rush beds

than to roam the banks of a clear chub river when it is full of summer weed, with the bare essentials of tackle and a few baits, looking for individual fish or small groups, manoeuvring into a casting position and getting the bait to the fish without causing any alarm. The first cast is always the best chance, often the only chance, for it either brings a fish or empties the swim.

Occasionally the bait may be cast accurately to roll down

Floating bait against flotsam raft is a chub killer

the current close to the fish, only to be ignored. In this case, having retrieved the bait well below the fish, a fresh cast should be made to drop the bait with a pronounced splash just behind the fish. Quite often the result is that the fish whips round to grab the bait instantly.

One of the special excitements of chub fishing is that in many rivers it is possible to fish in a style which allows one to watch the bait and see a fish approach and take it.

This is true to a large extent when fishing a floating crust bait, a method which is very effective on some rivers and would be anywhere if the chub saw enough floating crusts to be used to them.

It is always worth while to float a few crusts down the stream before starting to fish. This will often provoke a few fish to come to the surface, may show exactly where a feeding fish lies, and will at least demonstrate the path of the currents.

Crust baits can be really large, for a chub has a huge gape and will tackle very substantial portions.

A spot loved above all others by large solitary chub occurs where a trailing branch traps current-borne twigs, leaves, etc., until it builds up a large raft of flotsam. Here, concealed from above, accustomed to food items being carried down the flow, the chub is most easily and effectively approached by a bait which floats down naturally to come to rest against the upstream edge of the raft.

Chub are quite reliable night feeders, especially when the air is warm and the sky overcast. At such times they tend to move into shallow water to feed, perhaps no deeper than will barely cover them.

When fishing by night it is best to delay the start until it is fully dark and the fish have had time to relax some of their natural caution. One can then safely fish at rather closer range than is usually possible by day, and with less risk that the landing of one fish will scare the rest.

Ordinary legering, with or without weight according to the bait and the water conditions, detecting bites by holding the line with finger and thumb, is a style which will meet most situations very adequately. The baits which appeal to chub by day are usually equally effective by night.

Chub are good takers of a large, bushy dry fly

93

Dace (*Leuciscus leuciscus*)

Almost all rivers and many small streams hold dace in large numbers, but in few of them do the dace reach significant sizes. A fish of a pound can be reckoned as large. Small chub are quite often mistaken for large dace; dace, however, are readily identified by their slimmer shape, smaller mouth and the concave lower edge of the anal fin.

Apart from the few large fish, dace are usually found in extremely large shoals, occupying for most of the year the streamier stretches, and early in the season the shallow, rippling runs. From mid-autumn onwards they are likely to have moved into deeper and quieter water and to feed on or near to the bottom.

Those who find a special challenge in seeking the larger dace will generally fare better if they concentrate throughout on the deeper water of moderate current.

Dace are willing to eat a wide variety of anglers' baits, including all the bread-based items, hemp seed, maggots, small worms, etc., although seasonal and regional preferences may be evident.

Inevitably, through similarity of habits, dace often exist in competition with other species and are caught on tackle which is a great deal stronger than their size merits. There is much more fun, when dace shoals can be located, in fishing for them with tackle which makes no concession to the larger species which may come along. For this, truly sport fishing, a light, tip-actioned rod of 10–11 feet is ideal, with a line of as little as 1 lb. breaking strain, functioning pleasantly in the methods most suited to dace fishing.

Although dace will occasionally take quite large items of bait not intended for them and presented on large hooks, small items are usually much more successful in taking large catches from shoals, and a range of hook sizes from 14 to 18 will cover all dace fishing.

Due to their shoaling habit dace can often be caught very rapidly in very large numbers. This makes them a very popular fish with the match angler whose concern is to accumulate a high total weight.

The dace, a small shoal fish caught by most methods

Dace respond well to frequent light feeding

By far the most success with dace comes to baits which are presented at current speed either by swimming the stream or by very light long trotting.

Dace respond well to frequent light use of a fine cereal groundbait with bait samples added, say a walnut-size knob of groundbait and half a dozen maggots every one or two casts.

Maggots are usually as good as any other small bait for this kind of fishing, and are more convenient to use than most others. Hemp seed is very convenient to use but more prolonged loose feeding is called for to get the fish really interested.

Dace have a reputation for feeding in a way which calls for a very rapid strike, but though this may be true of very small fish it certainly is not true of all dace. Their bites may, however, be unpredictable and a strike should be made at any unusual float movement whether it be a tilt, a dip, a slight deviation from its course, as well as at more decisive indications.

In early summer, when dace shoals are often to be found concentrated in fast and shallow stretches, very interesting and testing fishing can be had by feeding floating maggot chrysalids down the stream until fish are seen to be taking them at the surface, and then sending down a similar bait with a very small float which is either self cocking or unweighted.

This brings very sharp bites of an unpredictable nature and demands a keen eye and a quick hand if a satisfactory proportion of bites are to result in fish.

Later in the season better results, and often better quality fish, are to be had by very light legering in deeper glides and near-slacks. The bait can usefully be a little larger, of paste or flake, or of fairly small worms.

When really cold conditions prevail and fish are feeding very briefly at long intervals, small cubes of crust, no more than $\frac{1}{4}''$ when dry, should be fished about an inch above the bottom. This often brings a few fish when nothing else will.

Crust cube, a good bait for larger dace

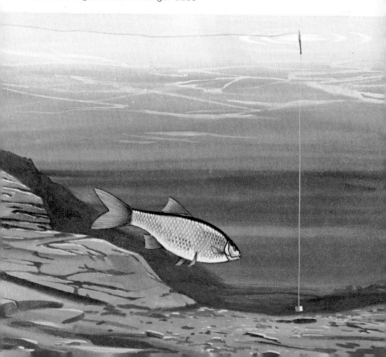

Eel (*Anguilla anguilla*)

The distribution of fresh-water eels is almost world-wide, covering every type of river and stream, and extending to lakes large and small, reservoirs and pools of all kinds even where there is no easy or direct connection with a watercourse.

The European eel grows to maturity in fresh water, reaching weights approaching ten-pounds, though half that is more common, taking seven or more years, before migrating two thirds of the way across the Atlantic to a spawning ground shared with eels from the North American continent. The larvae (lepto-cephali) then take as much as three years to return before ascending rivers as miniature adults (elvers).

The life cycle of the Australian eel follows a similar pattern, though their breeding area is believed to be in the Pacific Ocean. Eels are present in most Australian waters, very plentiful in some, but in spite of achieving impressive sizes, certainly up to around twenty pounds, attract little attention from anglers.

The eel's development from leptocephalus to adult

The eel is a muscular, powerful fish of great stamina and tenacity of life. It is virtually impossible to play an eel to exhaustion before landing it, as one can do with almost every other species, consequently an eel of even moderate size is a challenging quarry which calls for very robust tackle and unyielding tactics if it is to be kept from the sanctuary of weeds, roots, rock crevices, etc.

Eels are esentially piscivorous, feeding largely on the small fry of other species. They will also take frogs, newts, other small aquatic creatures and are enthusiastic scavengers for dead fish. Their greatest depredations stem from their great appetite for the spawn of other fish.

By day eels spend a great deal of their time concealed in submerged vegetation, crevices in timbering or stonework, etc., and, where the bottom is soft, in submerged burrows. They are always alert for prey, however, and are adept at picking off individual fish without alarming a shoal of fry. A great deal of their feeding takes place during darkness when they have a particular ability to locate food by scent.

The snake-like form of the eel commonly causes some

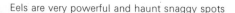

Eels are very powerful and haunt snaggy spots

degree of revulsion, but they provide a delicious and very nutritious food as well as being a worthy opponent for the angler.

Eels are caught on just about every bait in use by anglers but when fishing specifically for them no bait is more effective than small dead fish or large worms, fished stationary on the bottom.

Almost any fish, sea or freshwater, will attract eels, though there is probably some advantage in using a bait whose flesh is of an oily nature and piercing it several times to release body fluids into the water to act as an attractor. Bleak, gudgeon and sprats are of a convenient size, any local species is perfectly suitable, and portions of herring or mackerel also make good baits.

There is no advantage in using the traditional treble hook; there may indeed be a disadvantage in that it inevitably offers unengaged hook points for the eel to bite against and increases the difficulty of a secure hook-hold.

A large single hook of the highest quality, size 4 or 6, should be tucked into the angle of the bait's jaw with a short wire trace threaded through the bait from mouth to vent so as to fish the bait head-down on the hook. When conditions allow it the bait should be left unweighted to avoid offering resistance to a bite.

Worms are best fished in bunches, each worm being hooked once through its centre.

Eels are found in a wide range of water conditions; they

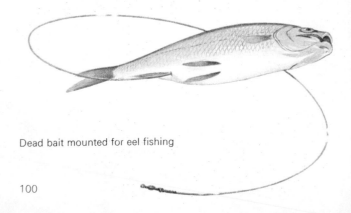

Dead bait mounted for eel fishing

are well able to cope with the rushing currents of weirs and falls but are completely at home in still water. Wherever one seeks eels, though, they are best looked for where there is adjacent cover in the form of weed growth, fallen trees, rocky ground, etc., for they love the dark and secret places.

There is no place for finesse in the landing of eels. Once line is being drawn steadily from the reel, a hard strike should lead into a hard heave to lift the eel from the bed, and once moving it should be kept coming by a pumping action. A powerful rod and a line of not less than 10 lb. breaking strain are essential if eels of more than a modest size are to be handled confidently.

All but the largest eels are best landed by being slid up the bank. When a landing net is used it must be very large, close meshed and very deep.

A piece of rough sacking simplifies gripping an eel for unhooking. If the eel is to be killed, though, it is best to do this first with a knife thrust through the base of the skull.

The eel is a powerful fish, calling for strong tackle

Grayling (*Thymallus thymallus*)

The grayling, although a relative of the salmonids, is judged by most British anglers as not truly a game fish. In some parts of the world it is accorded a higher status. It is, nevertheless, a fine sporting fish of handsome appearance which fights

Grayling like a lively, rippling stream

doggedly if not spectacularly, and its quality as a food fish is certainly no more than fractionally inferior to the best of trout. The grayling, said to smell of thyme, has a distinctive, large, sail-like dorsal fin and a marked irridescence on the flanks which rapidly fades after death.

This species is widely distributed through the rivers of Europe, the British Isles and North America, and thrives in the mountain streams of Australasia. It has a high tolerance for cold conditions, and commonly feeds in conditions which test the hardiness of the angler, for grayling fishing can well coincide with frost-bound banks and flurries of snow.

In general, the grayling's habits and tastes bring it into competition with trout, which leads to ruthless treatment in some high quality game rivers. It prefers the streamy water to the quiet stretches and is found over gravel and sand rather than silty parts.

The grayling, a beautiful fish and good eating

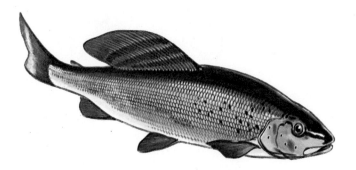

Providing other conditions are favourable, grayling will occupy quite shallow water during the warmer months, but during the colder weather they are best caught by bait fishing in fairly deep glides which have a moderate, even current.

There is a good choice of baits which appeal to grayling. They will feed freely on any kind of naturally occurring insect or larva, on grasshoppers, beetles, and caterpillars, and they will accept maggots, worms, and baits of bread.

It is said that grayling provide the best of guides to the well-being of a fishery. If they are thriving there can be little wrong with the quality of the water, for they will not tolerate any significant degree of pollution.

Many of the very best grayling rivers are more renowned as trout waters and little serious angling is done for the grayling. The similarity of their tastes and habits inevitably brings some grayling to the trout angler, however, and demonstrates that dry and wet fly fishing for grayling, exactly as used by the trout angler, is a rewarding approach.

Grayling give good sport on both bait and fly

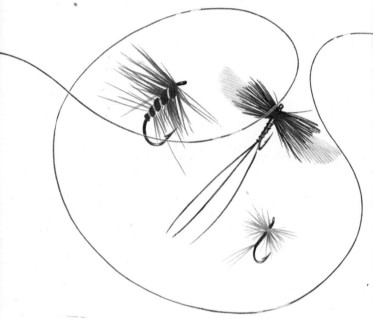

The choice of fly is not usually a critical matter for grayling are free takers of most imitative patterns in use for trout, and of small nymphs and wet flies of the attractor type.

Bait fishing for grayling is most popular in the smaller rivers of brisk current, with long rippling runs and stickles. The normal method is long trotting, the tackle being fed out to cover a long run of water with the bait travelling at current speed.

The lively character of typical grayling water has led to the popularity of a special design of float having a slightly bulbous body which enables it to ride fast rippling water.

Few rivers hold really large grayling, fish of 1–2 lb. would be reckoned very pleasing on most waters, and fairly light tackle can be used for bait fishing. A light hollow glass rod with line of 2–3 lb. breaking strain would be adequate and pleasant to use, and a range of hooks from size 10–14 would suit the range of baits.

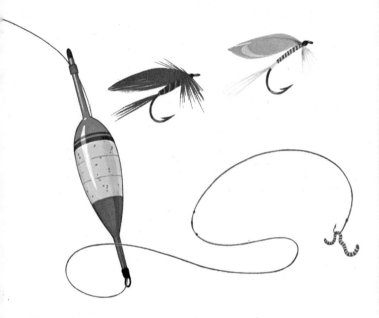

The traditional bait for grayling is a small worm, either a cockspur or a bandling, and these are undoubtedly attractive to grayling. Maggots are more readily obtainable in the large numbers which allow free feeding of the swim, a method which draws fish from a distance and stimulates feeding when they are dour.

In really hard conditions even the grayling are likely to fall back into deeper and steadier currents where baits fished on the bed or very close to it are advisable.

The gudgeon, a favourite with
small boys, very useful as a bait
for larger species

Gudgeon (*Gobio gobio*)

This small member of the carp family, looking rather like a
small barbel, and rarely exceeding 4 ounces in weight, is
found in most European rivers where it favours gravelly
stretches with a moderate flow. It also thrives in some
enclosed still waters.

It is not a fish of great importance to the angler except that
it can usually be relied upon to provide some small sport
when more impressive species will not respond. It does
have some importance in the diet of the predatory species
and makes an excellent bait for large chub and for perch and
pike.

Gudgeon were highly esteemed for their delicate flavour
and are still a popular dish in parts of France.

This little fish is completely omnivorous and feeds almost
entirely on the bottom. Traditionally, gudgeon fishing was
preceded and interspersed by a vigorous raking of the bed
to send down a cloud of silt and to release larvae and other
small creatures, thus gathering a large concentration of fish.

This preparation is most effective in shallow streamy water
and can conveniently be used by the angler standing in the

water of a shallow ford, fishing directly down the current, and scuffling the bed with his feet from time to time.

Alternatively, a fine cereal groundbait with added sand can be used to achieve the same effect.

To find any pleasure in catching gudgeon one must use the finest of tackle, ignoring the possibility of larger species. The line cannot be too fine and hooks of size 16 or 18 will suit all baits.

Maggots and maggot chrysalids are excellent baits which can conventiently be trickled into the stream whilst fishing. Stewed wheat and hemp grains make attractive baits of suitable size, and very small cockspur worms, or pieces of worm, are probably as effective as any other bait. All the bread baits, in suitable sizes, are also accepted freely.

Few anglers fish specifically for gudgeon except when they are wanted as bait, but to the match angler they can represent a worthwhile addition to his catch when they are present in large numbers.

Raking the bed to attract gudgeon

All the perch family are hunters of small fish

Perch (*Perca fluviatilis*)

The European perch, a gregarious predator, is a popular sporting fish found in rivers and lakes throughout the British Isles and Europe. It commonly achieves weights up to 2–4 lb., though it breeds so prolifically that in many waters dwarfing occurs through gross over-population.

Known locally as the English perch or Redfin, this species was introduced to Australian waters a century ago and now thrives in rivers, lagoons and reservoirs. Here it is fished for with baits of small fish, prawns, grubs, etc., and with flies and artificial lures of all kinds. In the Australian environment the perch grows very large with weights of 4–5 lb. being common and specimens of 20 lb. on record.

The distinctive feature of the colouration of perch is the broad, almost black banding descending from the spine down the flanks. This well befits their habit of resting in the con-

cealment of reeds, rushes, etc. to prey upon such small fish and other creatures as come within striking distance. The perch is not a particularly fast swimmer, preferring always to strike from ambush.

River perch are usually found over gravelly beds in water of moderate flow where plant growth or other concealment is available. They are especially fond of undercut banks and are often to be found alongside timbering or masonry.

During the early part of the season and occasionally at other times, they may assemble in groups to harass shoals of fry and minnows, working with apparent organisation and roaming the water in search of easy feeding. This activity is readily observed, with small fry leaping from the water and pursuing perch causing obvious disturbance.

Small perch often occur in very large shoals, especially in extensive still waters, but the larger specimens are rarely found other than in very small groups and often as solitary fish monopolising a favourable situation.

Left : small mouth bass. Right : large mouth bass

Australia has several indigenous perches, which have the typical perch form, differing mainly in size, colouration and distribution.

The Murray river system holds the so-called Murray cod, a mainly predacious and scavenging fish which reaches very large sizes, with the rod-caught record standing at 90 lb. This is fished for with baits of frogs, crayfish, mussels, worms and meaty baits and is also taken commercially both in nets and on lines.

The golden perch is a somewhat smaller fish with a wider distribution embracing the Murray and Dawson river systems and very many creeks, lakes and swamps. This, too, has the typically predacious nature of the perch family and is angled for with baits of shrimps, worms, etc., as well as being taken on spinners and plugs and on artificial flies. Fish of 40 lb. are on record, with the rod-caught record standing at 11 lb.

The silver perch, with a distribution similar to that of the golden perch, is a shoal fish taken in large numbers both by anglers and commercial fishermen. If favours baits of prawns, shrimps, worms, and similar small creatures and is taken also on flies and lures.

North America has its own indigenous yellow perch (*Perca flavescens*) very widely distributed throughout vast lakes and river systems. This is a very popular anglers' fish, often caught in very large numbers and well-esteemed as a food fish. This fish is much sought by lure fishing, a small wobbling minnow plug being a popular choice, and by using small fish as bait.

The same continent also has the large mouth and small mouth black basses, also members of the perch family, renowned sporting and edible fishes, which have been introduced to a few European waters. These are sought by bait, lure and fly fishing.

The angler who fishes for perch in rivers must first concern himself with finding where the fish are, for although some favourable spots are usually reliable, a stretch which holds fish one day may well be empty the next.

Unless the perch are betraying their whereabouts by their activity they are best found by mobile, exploratory angling, either dropping a worm or minnow into likely areas or making a few casts with a small, bright spinner and watching for pursuing perch. Once a perch is caught or seen it is usually safe to assume that more are in the vicinity and to settle down to their catching.

Once perch have been located simple float fishing is a very satisfactory method as it allows easy adjustment of depth of fishing. This can be a crucial factor, for perch will unpredictably choose to feed at depths varying between just sub-surface to hard on the bed.

There is rarely a more effective bait than worms and although small varieties may occasionally be preferred, large lobworms usually bring the best results. The worm should be hooked once through its middle, and a little time given before striking.

In weeded waters, where clear channels run between dense cover, the bait should be offered as close to the weed as possible. A scattering of broken worms in and around the weeds will encourage the perch to emerge and feed where they can more easily be caught.

Paternoster tackle is ideal for use where the bait has to be dropped into small areas of clear water and offered clear of the bed, and for fishing a live minnow so that it is free to swim around within the radius of the hook link. It is also the perfect style for lowering a bait beneath vertical or undercut banks. The rod should be hand-held all the time, a little line being given on a bite to reduce the resistance of a tight line against the rod tip.

When it is necessary to search for fish the bait should be offered near to weeds, rushes, timber work, undercut banks, etc., for perch which are not actively hunting will surely be using their camouflaged markings to lie in ambush.

The perch fishing in very small ponds is usually of poor quality due to prolific breeding and restricted food supply.

Above: basic perch tackle. Below: paternostering near the bank

Float fishing for short range, legering for distance
Inset: double minnow, an excellent perch bait

There are, however, generally a few notably large fish which prey on their fellows; these are best caught on live baits of some size. Large lakes, reservoirs and gravel pits generally offer the best prospects of big fish in numbers.

Once again location of the fish is the primary problem. If one remembers that the principal food of sizeable perch consists of small fish, the problem may be half solved if shoals of minnows or fry can be found. Otherwise one has to choose between a mobile approach which searches for the fish, and remaining in a favourable area in the hope that fish will come to it.

During the warmer months perch will generally be found in the warmer water of the relatively shallow areas and will favour the windward side. Here, if the distance is not too great, straightforward float fishing with worm bait will soon demonstrate if perch are about. If very small perch are caught there is little chance of larger fish, since perch shoals generally consist of fish of much the same size.

During cold weather the shallows and surface layers are not likely to hold fish. Attention should now be concentrated on deeper water, though in very deep lakes the absolute depths are not usually productive at any time.

In really large waters legering enables the coverage of more water due to the longer casts which can be made. The weight should be of a free-sliding type for perch are quick to drop a bait if undue drag is felt, and arrangement should be made for a few feet of line to be freely drawn on a bite.

When a static bait brings no results, it is worth trying a slow retrieve along the bed, just a foot at a time with a pause between. The movement of the bait is an added attraction and the silt cloud may well draw a patrolling fish to the bait.

Two small minnows, lip hooked together, make a better bait than a single large one, as movement is maintained and there is no tendency to burrow into weed.

Spinning, either with an artificial lure or with a dead fish, imitates most closely the natural diet of mature perch.

Any fish of suitable size can be used, from about two inches up to about five inches. It may be mounted simply by

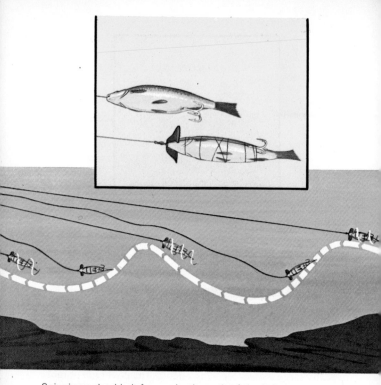

Spinning a dead bait for perch : the path of the bait

threading the line from mouth to vent, no wire trace being needed, and tying on a suitable treble hook. Thus mounted, the bait will swoop, dive and spiral erratically as the tackle is manipulated.

Alternatively it can be mounted on a spinning flight equipped with vanes to make it revolve. For deep fishing the flight can incorporate a leaded spike which is thrust down the throat of the bait.

A mounted fish should not be merely cast out and retrieved directly, but should be brought back in irregular movements of varying speed so as to lift, dive, twist and dart in its passage through the water.

Very many patterns of lures are successful with perch:

devon minnows, bar spoons, wagtails, plugs, jigs, and so on in all their variations. Any lure which works vigorously and has plenty of flash and movement will attract this most inquisitive and agressive fish, and it can well be a fairly large lure too, for many perch have been taken on lures intended for larger species. As with a dead fish, the lure should be retrieved in a way which imparts a wide range of obstrusive movements.

When taking spun baits and lures perch will usually hook themselves, but a strike should be given as soon as a fish is felt, though it should be of only moderate force for the mouth of a perch, being widely extensile, is easily torn.

A refinement and added attraction to spinning with both artificial lures and dead fish baits can be made by adding a bright, flashy hookless spoon some three or four feet up-trace from the lure proper. This, with a sight-hunting species like perch, much increases the chances that fish will be attracted, especially when fishing deep or murky water.

Perch respond to vigorous movement and flash

Pike (*Esox lucius*)

The pikes, long-bodied, flat-snouted predators, are confined to the Northern hemisphere, being widely distributed through the waters of Europe, Northern Asia and North America. The monster of the pikes is the American Muskellunge (*Esox masquinongy*) which can reach a weight of 100 lb., the more common *Esox lucius* achieving about half that weight in favourable conditions.

When still very small pike turn from eating invertebrates to a diet of fish, and large pike are known also to devour water fowl and aquatic mammals.

The flanks of the pike are beautifully camouflaged to suit its habit of lying concealed against vegetation before dashing out to seize its prey. Generally taken crosswise and severely bitten by the many sharp teeth, the prey is then turned to be swallowed head first, sometimes after being first carried back to the lair.

In spite of its fierce appearance, however, and its efficiency at obtaining its food, the pike does not deserve the ruthless, even cruel, treatment it sometimes receives. Its killing of other fish is restricted entirely to what it needs to eat, and though it may need to be removed from some stocked fisheries, it is probable that its presence is of general benefit in many over-populated waters. Its sporting potential, too, is some justification for its depredations among the smaller species.

Pike are most commonly taken by variations of three methods: live baiting, dead baiting and spinning with artificial lures. Exceptionally they are taken on large flies.

A quarry such as the pike, even in waters where it reaches no more than half its potential weight, clearly merits robust tackle. A rod of 9–10 feet, in built cane or glass, powerful enough to throw a half-pound fish bait, will cope adequately with whatever a pike may do subsequently, and a line of 10–15 lb. breaking strain is not too heavy unless the pike are known to run small. High quality hooks are needed to withstand the crushing bite of a bony mouth and a wire trace is needed for confident handling of any size of pike.

The pike, perfectly adapted for a predatory life

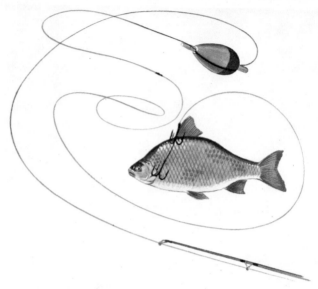

Live baiting, a traditional and effective style

Live baiting, probably the oldest method of catching pike, has lost some of its popularity in recent years, due in part to a growing concern with the ethics of using live fish as bait and in part to great developments in other methods. Nevertheless pike have not stopped feeding on live fish and this bait will always catch pike for those who wish to use it.

In its usual form live baiting involves float tackle, with the bait being encouraged to swim around so as to cover a large expanse of water. The float should not be of such bulk as will restrict unduly the mobility of the bait, two small, streamlined floats often being preferred to one large one.

Most anglers have their own ideas on how the hooks should be placed, the most popular method being to nick one treble hook in the base of the dorsal fin with a second placed at the base of the gill opening. One really large single hook is preferred by some anglers who maintain that hooking is cleaner and more certain when only one point can be engaged.

In shallow water and moderate depths there is no call for weight on the line; it is more important to allow full mobility of the bait. When pike are found in deep water, however, a suitable weight must hold the bait at fishing depth below a sliding float. In very deep water float fishing becomes cumbersome, and it is better to turn to leger or paternoster tackle.

All styles of live bait fishing pose the problem of timing the strike so as to ensure that the bait and hooks are properly within the pike's mouth so as to engage securely yet have not been swallowed so far as to cause lethal hooking. Many formulae have been suggested, but none is likely always to succeed and each angler must decide for himself on which side of the ideal timing he wishes to err.

Live baiting should not be allowed to become a static waiting game. Better results usually come to those who regard

Live baits offered at various depths

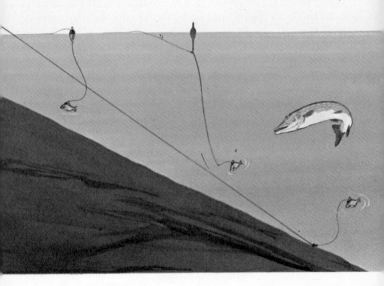

One method of hooking a fish for dead baiting

it as merely another method of searching those areas which their knowledge of pike tells to be promising.

Pike are often drawn to a concentration of small fish and good results sometimes come following a spell of ground-baiting to attract the food species to the vicinity of the bait.

The reduced popularity of live bait fishing has seen a simultaneous increase in the use of dead fish as pike baits and a general acceptance that, properly used, they are as effective as live baits in some waters.

Only within recent years has it become widely appreciated that pike are scavengers as well as predators, taking stationary dead fish from the bed and well able to locate them by scent as well as sight.

Any fish of suitable size can be used, either of a local or a marine species. Herring and mackerel are convenient and attractive, their oily nature ensuring a good scent trial.

A small pike, up to two or three pounds in weight, is reckoned a very good bait for really large pike. Such a bait would need to be thrown out by hand or by using a suitable stick.

Better results may come to a dead bait which is twitched very slowly along the bed

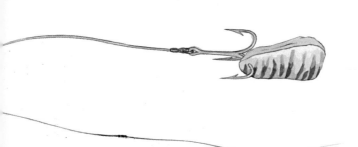

Some advantage is undoubtedly gained by groundbaiting with chopped fish, preferably in lines radiating from the fishing spot.

The dead fish bait is fished head-down, on a wire trace, and is usually armed with at least two treble hooks, one set either in the angle of the jaw or in the gill slit, the other mid-way down the flank. The tail of the bait should be bound to the trace with a few turns of fuse wire or thread.

Except when fishing in rivers of considerable flow no weight should be used; provided the bait has had its swim bladder burst, it will sink under its own weight.

In still waters a known or suspected feeding ground should be fished; in rivers likely spots are at the head of a long steady glide or in a quiet eddy at the edge of a good run of current. Adjacent rushes or other weed is always a good sign.

A float can be used to indicate bites but it is more usual to allow line to be freely drawn by the pike. A buzzer indicator is very convenient with this style.

In very cold weather when the pike are lying in deep water, better results often come to a dead bait which is moved along the bed just a very few inches every few minutes.

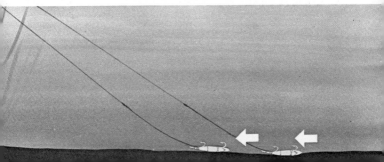

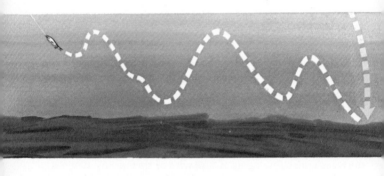

Mobile dead baiting, the path of the retrieve

A dead fish can also be used to good effect in a number of ways which make it appear living and enable the coverage of a large expanse of water when pike have to be searched for.

In this case the bait, of any desired size from a few inches upwards, is threaded with a baiting needle to fish head up the trace. With fairly small baits one treble hook at the vent is sufficient; with larger baits an additional hook, either single or treble, inserted into the head, will carry the bait more securely as well as giving a better hooking potential. The lips of the bait should be bound together around the trace for greater durability.

Sprats are a popular and effective small bait, rather fragile but very bright and attractive, suitable for use on fairly light spinning tackle. Herrings and local species of similar size are better handled on a light surf casting rod designed to cast weights of 6–10 ounces.

The bait is cast out, successive casts being fanned out to cover the water, and allowed time to sink slowly near to the bed before the retrieve is commenced. A lift of the rod and a few turns of the reel will bring the bait swooping upwards towards the surface, when it should be allowed to sink again, twisting and flashing.

A straight, even retrieve is much less effective in luring pike than one in which life is imparted to the bait by working the rod and varying the speed of retrieve.

When pike are deep in the water a carrot-shaped lead attached to the trace and thrust down the bait's throat will keep the bait well submerged. In high summer, when weed near the surface presents a problem, the bait can be made to ride high, breaking the surface, by inserting a piece of expanded polystyrene.

Casts fanned out to search the water

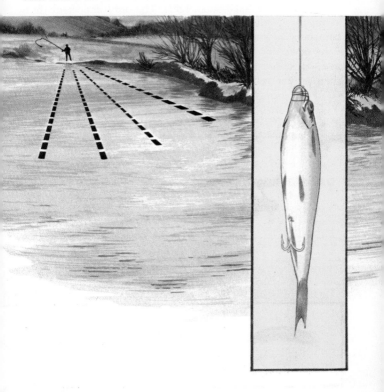

A variation of this method, giving close control in restricted conditions, is to use a small bait with enough weight inserted to sink it quite rapidly. This is fished at close range in a sink-and-draw style, following a sharply zig-zagging course between surface and bed, always moving, twisting, flashing, in a way which pike cannot resist.

Pike are taken freely on an enormous range of artificial lures – revolving and vibrating spoons in sizes from an inch or so up to around a foot, plugs of every type, wagtails, devons, jigs, and so on – some universally popular, some favoured only locally, all affording an effective, active and skilful form of angling.

The tackle in popular use shows marked regional variation, ranging from 5 foot wands with a cranked handle for use with small multiplying reels, to powerful rods of 10 feet or more used with large fixed spool reels. The only important thing about the tackle is that it should allow the angler confident control in the conditions he encounters in his fishing.

In most still waters, where temperature stratification is marked, summer conditions commonly find the pike seeking their prey in relatively shallow water and in the warmer sur-

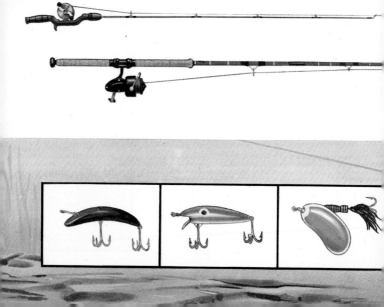

face layers. At this time the most successful lures are likely to be those of low density and vigorous action at low recovery speeds, such as vibrating spoons, shallow running plugs, surface poppers, and similar designs.

Unless they are seen to be actively hunting, as they do occasionally, the retrieve should bring the lure as close as possible to weed growth rushes, etc., where pike are likely to be lying, and should be of varying speed with the lure darting, hesitating, sometimes breaking the surface.

In colder conditions, and at any time in deep lakes where the food species are bottom-living, pike may be at depths which require a different range of lures for effective angling. Deep-running jointed plugs of large size, and large heavy spoons with a throbbing action are reliable for deep fishing, either cast from the shore or trolled deeply behind a slowly moving boat.

Lures have an inherent fascination for most anglers and many treasure a collection as much for its own sake as for its usefulness. It should be remembered, however, that it is usually much more important where and how the lure is used than what its pattern is.

Pike are caught on a vast range of artificial lures

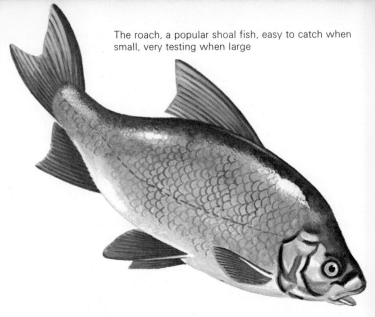
The roach, a popular shoal fish, easy to catch when small, very testing when large

Roach (*Rutilus rutilus*)

The European roach, a shoal fish of the carp family, is found in most waters throughout Western Europe. It is tolerant of a very wide range of conditions and will thrive in fast flowing streams, sluggish rivers, large lakes and reservoirs, small ponds and canals, in some cases in spite of considerable pollution.

It is an omnivorous feeder with a diet of shrimps, larvae, leeches, crustacea and smaller aquatic organisms, berries, seeds, soft weeds, and in some popular waters a major item of food is that which anglers use in its pursuit.

In many waters roach abound in great numbers, are dwarfed to a fraction of their potential size, and are caught with great ease in large numbers. In fewer fisheries they grow to nearer their maximum size, with some fish of weights between 2 and $3\frac{1}{2}$ lb., are very difficult to tempt and are rarely caught.

The roach in each type of water need to be approached almost as a different species, having different habits and diets, and requiring a different approach from the angler. Large

fish from the bank, a long rod is advisable as it allows better placement of the bait and gives closer control of hooked fish in restricted and snaggy water

It is possible sometimes to pin-point the position of individual fish as they burrow into weed roots and suck at weeds and rushes, by watching for shaking or vibrating of emergent growth. When this is seen an accurately placed bait will often bring a quick response.

In beds of lilies the lifting or shaking of leaves can show where tench are sucking small organisms from the underside. When they are so engaged they readily take a small red worm flicked in to fall slowly among the leaves.

When tench are browsing among weed growth they will sometimes take food right at the surface. A few small pieces of crust, floated into the weeds, should precede the crust bait.

The fact is that there are very few times when it is pointless to fish for tench if one is prepared to vary the method, the bait, the pitch, to seek out the fish and devise a style to appeal.

The pike-perches: Zander (*Lucioperca lucioperca*); Wall-eye (*Stizostedion vitreum*)

The zander, a species of European origin, and the related wall-eye of Eastern North America, both have the slim body shape of the pike and the spined dorsal fin of the perch. Once of limited distribution, their value as a sporting fish has encouraged their introduction to fresh waters.

From the angler's point of view there is little point in distinguishing between the two pike-perches except that in its native country the wall-eye reaches weights up to 25 lb., about double the weight reached by the zander. Their habits, however, show no significant differences, both being basically predacious but also scavenging, both appearing to thrive equally well in running or still water.

Pike-perch have been caught accidentally on many baits intended for other species, especially on worms, but angling methods are best based on the fact that the main item of natural diet for adult fish consists of small fish.

The pike-perches: above, the zander; below, the wall-eye

The pike-perches, basically predators, are best fished for with live or dead fish baits

A live bait can suitably be from 3 inches upwards, of any convenient species, armed with either a large single hook or a treble. This can be floated, legered or free lined, preferably alongside marginal herbage or submerged weed, bearing in mind that predators are often most easily located by reference to the habits of the species upon which they prey.

The pike-perch is equally willing to accept dead baits fished stationary on the bed. It seems probable that scent plays a part in the attraction of this bait and there is some advantage in piercing the bait several times.

Also attractive to pike-perch are all artificial lures, both those which represent fish and other creatures and those which are purely attractors, spoons, plugs, jigs, streamers, and so on, fished exactly as for other predatory species.

The pike-perch is an attractive fish and a sizeable quarry which warrants the use of substantial tackle.

Trap and net for catching small bait fish

Catfish, burbot, small species

Very many catfishes exist throughout the world, all having the long barbules which have given them their name.

One of the largest is the wels (*Silurus glanis*), a native of Europe's major rivers, which has been introduced to a number of English lakes where weights of more than thirty pounds have been recorded.

North America has several catfishes, of which one, the brown bullhead, has been introduced to European rivers.

Catfish are widely distributed in the Murray-Darling river system of Australia where they reach weights up to 15 lb. and are angled for with baits of shrimps, worms, grubs, etc.

Largely, but not entirely, nocturnal, catfish use their sensitive barbules to locate food, and are best fished for with baits of large worms or small dead fish. Robust tackle is called for.

Burbot, the only freshwater cod, is a fish of rather eel-like form which occurs from Northern Asia and Central Europe to North America. Once thought extinct in British rivers, several burbot have recently been caught on bottom-fished baits. It is not, however, fished for specifically.

The many species whose small size makes them of little real interest to anglers are nevertheless of great importance to the well-being of a fishery, forming an important link in the food chain of larger species. It is rare, for example, to find a minnow-rich water which does not also hold some fish grown large on a diet of minnows. This most common of small fishes makes an excellent bait for perch, chub and barbel.

The slim, pale bleak, common in most European rivers, shoals near the surface and is readily caught on small baits and fine tackle. A dead bleak makes the best of eel baits and is large enough to appeal to pike.

Loaches of many kinds exist throughout Europe and Asia, the commonest being the stone loach. These are easily caught by turning over stones in shallow water and make an excellent bait for perch and chub.

It is well to know the habits and distribution of the small species, for this knowledge will often help in the location of the larger fish which feed on them.

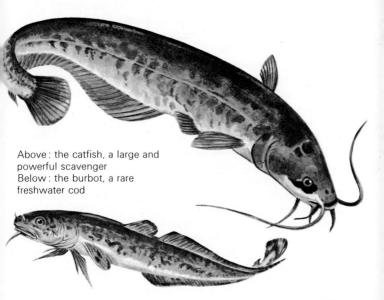

Above: the catfish, a large and powerful scavenger
Below: the burbot, a rare freshwater cod

Many European anglers find a special appeal in match fishing

Match Fishing

The introduction of a competitive element into angling, with financial reward for the successful and sometimes with gambling on the result, is peculiarly European.

Matches are usually 'pegged-down', the angler being strictly restricted to the short stretch he is allocated by draw, but roving is sometimes permitted. They may be fished to River Authority size limits or 'all-in', there may be restrictions on baits and tackle, the result may rest solely on total weight caught or on a points system which also takes account of the number of fish.

The match angler needs to know the water he fishes, to be clear at the start how he proposes to fish and what species he aims for, for he cannot afford to waste much of his limited time in experiment. Sheer speed and economy of movement are important, and match anglers develop dexterity and tackle control to a very high degree.

Most match angling is done with light, hollow glass rods with a tip action which facilities fast striking, using lines in the range 1–3 lbs. and hooks ranging down to size 20 and even smaller. This is the tackle which is best suited to very rapid catching, at short range, of very many small fish, the approach which wins the majority of matches.

Until recent years most match angling was done with a small, delicately-shotted float, swimming the stream, but the swing tip indicator has gained much popularity especially in the broader rivers where bream are present.

Groundbaiting is of great importance to the match angler, not only that he may concentrate fish in his allotted short stretch and catch them without wasted time, but also that they are denied to his neighbours. In most well-stocked waters a handful of cereal mixture, with samples of the hook bait, will be used to almost every cast.

The standard baits are maggots and their chrysalids at the stage when they will sink, for these are baits which will be taken by all species large and small. Some anglers specialise in the fishing of 'bloodworms' on extremely fine tackle and tiny hooks.

Match angling is criticised on the grounds that it introduces considerations which cannot be reconciled with true angling for sport, but it cannot be denied that it is a branch of angling which appeals to very many thousands of anglers and that success in match fishing comes only to those who have developed and refined the basic skills to a very high degree.

The weigh-in at the end of a match

The specimen hunter takes care to conceal himself

Specimen Hunting

In direct opposition to the match angler, whose concern is to accumulate fish no matter what their size, the specimen hunter concerns himself exclusively with fish of a size which makes them noteworthy for their species, often concentrating his attention on a single favoured species.

During the past decade the formation of specimen hunting groups has been a remarkable feature of British angling. They now abound, many of them consisting rather informally of a handful of members with similar interests, but some with very many members, all affiliated to the National Association of Specimen Groups.

Their belief is that by discussion, by planned and concerted effort, by shared information and pooled experience, they are able more quickly and more completely to solve problems, explore waters, develop techniques so that they are able to choose venues, times, methods, baits, etc., which

make more nearly certain the catching of 'specimen' fish.

Information of all kinds is amassed, collated, analysed and circulated to members for their benefit and comment, it being maintained that in this way each member has available the results of a range of experiment greater than he could himself accumulate in a lifetime of angling.

In addition to the formally constituted groups there are many individual anglers whose specific aim is to catch only the larger fish, adapting tackle, baits, techniques, to this aim, and being ready to devote unlimited time to observation and exploration, waiting for the few notably large fish which make it all worth while.

All anglers would prefer to catch large fish rather than small, but most would rather catch small fish than nothing. The true specimen hunter, however, would rather not catch the small fish, believing that he thereby increases his chances of a subsequent large one. To him the catching of a notably large fish justifies extensive travel, a great deal of time and often considerable expense, and sustains his dedication through repeated disappointment.

The summing up

Man has always sought to capture fish for food and one suspects that even the primitive hunter whose survival depended upon success must have found a challenge and a deep satisfaction in the catching of fish. His reasons may be less compelling today, but the challenge remains stimulating and absorbing and the satisfaction deep, for there is in most of us a streak of atavism which relishes the pitting of human wits against the superior senses and protective instincts of the wild. Hence the countless millions the world over to whom angling is more than a mere pastime or hobby, meeting a need more elemental than amusement or pleasure.

The best of anglers are invariably those who approach their angling as hunters, having a deep understanding of the ways of their quarry, a sympathy with the natural world and an abiding concern for its ultimate welfare. They are, in fact, naturalists who happen also to be anglers.

Such men never fall into the error of under-estimating the ability of fish to detect potential danger and to learn by experience; they keep low and quiet, they move slowly and smoothly only when they must, they position themselves with due regard for cover and are in every way unobtrusive observers.

They are more than mere catchers of fish, to whom success is all. They are thinkers, experimenters, innovators, who are not content to wait for luck to favour them, but take steps to deserve it.

They know, too, that to catch no fish is not a failure. They fish for the sheer fun, the challenge and the total happiness of doing it, and to find these rewards does not demand that one should always catch fish. Nevertheless, they are not complacent or easily satisfied but realise the limitations of their knowledge and seek assiduously to extend it.

All anglers, however, the world over, successful or not, share the sport which above all others will remain engrossing and demanding, as well as rewarding, all their lives. I can wish them no more than that they find in their sport something near to the happiness which I have found.

The paraphernalia and the fish

BOOKS TO READ

Angling in Earnest by F. J. Taylor. MacGibbon and Kee, 1969.
Encyclopedia of Angling by A. N. Marston. Hamlyn, 1969.
Gravel Pit Fishing by T. Housby. Barrie and Jenkins, 1968.
Carp by J. Gibbinson. Macdonald, 1969.
All About Angling by J. Piper. Pelham Books, 1970.
The Angler's Year edited by P. Wheat. Pelham (annual).
Specimen Fish by P. Stone. Barrie and Jenkins, 1969.
Freshwater Fishing by B. Venables. Barrie and Jenkins, 1967.
Coarse Fishing for Absolute Beginners by E. Barnes. Studio Vista,
    1964
Catch a Big Fish by D. C. Forbes. Newnes, 1967.
Coarse Fishing by P. Stone. Brockhampton Press, 1969.
Fishing as we find it by P. Wheat. Warne, 1967.
Irish Coarse Fishing by J. Williams. Black, 1968.
Big Pike by G. Bucknall. Benn, 1965.
Bream and Barbel by P. Stone. Benn, 1964.
The Fighting Barbel by P. Wheat. Benn, 1967.
Fishing Tackle by D. Orton. Hamlyn, 1970.
River Fishing by C. Gamble. Hamlyn, 1970.

INDEX

Page numbers in bold type
refer to illustrations

SOME OTHER TITLES IN THIS SERIES

■ **Arts**
Antique Furniture/Architecture/Art Nouveau for Collectors/Clocks and Watches/Glass for Collectors/Jewellery/Musical Instruments/Porcelain/Pottery/Silver for Collectors/Victoriana

■ **Domestic Animals and Pets**
Budgerigars/Cats/Dog Care/Dogs/Horses and Ponies/Pet Birds/Pets for Children/Tropical Freshwater Aquaria/Tropical Marine Aquaria

■ **Domestic Science**
Flower Arranging

■ **Gardening**
Chrysanthemums/Garden Flowers/Garden Shrubs/House Plants/Plants for Small Gardens/Roses

■ **General Information**
Aircraft/Arms and Armour/Coins and Medals/Espionage/Flags/Fortune Telling/Freshwater Fishing/Guns/Military Uniforms/Motor Boats and Boating/National Costumes of the world/Orders and Decorations/Rockets and Missiles/Sailing/Sailing Ships and Sailing Craft/Sea Fishing/Trains/Veteran and Vintage Cars/Warships

■ **History and Mythology**
Age of Shakespeare/Archaeology/Discovery of: Africa/The American West/Australia/Japan/North America/South America/Great Land Battles/Great Naval Battles/Myths and Legends of: Africa/Ancient Egypt/Ancient Greece/Ancient Rome/India/The South Seas/Witchcraft and Black Magic

■ **Natural History**
The Animal Kingdom/Animals of Australia and New Zealand/Animals of Southern Asia/Bird Behaviour/Birds of Prey/Butterflies/Evolution of Life/Fishes of the world/Fossil Man/A Guide to the Seashore/Life in the Sea/Mammals of the world/Monkeys and Apes/Natural History Collecting/The Plant Kingdom/Prehistoric Animals/Seabirds/Seashells/Snakes of the world/Trees of the world/Tropical Birds/Wild Cats

■ **Popular Science**
Astronomy/Atomic Energy/Chemistry/Computers at Work/The Earth/Electricity/Electronics/Exploring the Planets/Heredity/The Human Body/Mathematics/Microscopes and Microscopic Life/Physics/Psychology/Undersea Exploration/The Weather Guide